Praise for

This I Accomplish: Harriet Powers'
Bible Quilt and Other Pieces

"After exploring a dated and obscure paper trail and recording the testimony of surviving individuals connected with the quilts, Kyra E. Hicks painstakingly documents the strange and wondrous journey taken by the two known nineteenth-century Harriet Powers quilts.

"Did Harriet Powers stitch magic protective charms into her Bible quilts? Once her quilted treasures left the care of this nineteenth-century African American woman of limited financial means, they were passed from one set of caring hands to another. During times when black-made artifacts were undervalued and even derided, Powers' quilts remained safe and secure. Hicks methodically documents the very colorful cast of nineteenth- and twentieth-century men and women who found themselves under the benevolent spell of the Powers quilts.

"Essential reading for anyone interested in Harriet Powers!"

Patricia A. Turner, author of *Crafted Lives:*
Stories and Studies of African American Quilters

"Fascinating!

"From the opening words of this book to the closing ones…a spellbinding tale is woven.

"*This I Accomplish* is a masterpiece of scholarship and detective work. The amount of research Kyra E. Hicks has done to unravel mysteries and her willingness to follow even the slightest lead is astonishing. You will be amazed and intrigued by the previously unknown information she uncovers."

Gwendolyn Magee, quilter and 2007
United States Artists Fellow

This I Accomplish: Harriet Powers' Bible Quilt and Other Pieces
Quilt Histories, Exhibition Lists, Annotated Bibliography and Timeline of a Great African American Quilter

by Kyra E. Hicks

Foreword by Bill Gaskins

Black Threads Press

ISBN: 978-0-9824796-5-0

Library of Congress Control Number: 2009904675

Library of Congress subject headings:
1. Powers, Harriet, 1837-1910— Biography
2. African American quilts—Bibliography
3. African American quiltmakers—Georgia
4. Quilting – United States—History
5. Quilts – Georgia—Athens

Cover Art: "Taking In Harriet Powers' Bible Quilt" by Linda Apple
See more of her work at www.AppleArts.com.

Cover Design: ManjariGraphics

Edited by Kristin P. Walinski, Scribe On Demand Editorial Services

Dedicated to

Barbara Imes Jorden & Jacqueline Imes Jenkins,
Co-founders of the
African American Ebony Rainbow Quilters Guild
of Gloucester County, New Jersey

and

In loving memory of

my Dad, Richard Wayne Hicks, Sr. (1934 – 2007),
Aunt Mimi, Mildred M. Jones (1920 – 2007),
Big Anita, Anita Joyce Hicks Kidd (1946 – 2007),
Great Aunt Alzeda, Alzeda Crockett Hacker (1907 – 2007),
Aunt Mary, Mary Elizabeth Hicks Ford (1936 – 2008), and
my Godmother, Arrilla Lovelace McZeal (1922 – 2008)

When the Lord finished speaking to Moses on Mount Sinai, he gave him the two tablets of the Testimony, the tablets of stone inscribed by the finger of God.
Exodus 31: 18

This I Accomplish: Harriet Powers' Bible Quilt and Other Pieces

Contents

ACKNOWLEDGMENTS 8

FOREWORD 10

INTRODUCTION 11

THE BIBLE QUILT 13
    Quilt Block Descriptions 14
    Exhibition History 15
    They Touched the *Bible Quilt* 17
        Jennie Smith (1862—1946) *19*
        Clara R. Jemison (1869—1907) *30*
        Lorene Curtis Diver (1846—1922) *31*
        Harriet A. Powers (1837—1910) *37*
        Lucine Finch (1875—1947) *48*
        Harold M. Heckman (1899—1987) *55*

THE PICTORIAL QUILT 62
    Quilt Block Descriptions 63
    Exhibition History 64
    Chain of Custody—Those Who Cared for the *Pictorial Quilt* 66
        Dr. Charles Cuthbert Hall (1852—1908) *66*
        Rev. Basil Douglas Hall (1888—1979) *74*
        Maxim Karolik (1893—1963) *81*
        A Young Artist Adds to the Pictorial Quilt *100*

BIBLIOGRAPHY 104
    Major Works about Harriet Powers and Her Quilts 104
    Books and Exhibit Catalogs 113
    Magazines, Journals and Newsletter Articles 125
    Newspapers 127
    Dissertations, Theses, Manuscripts and Papers 137
    Plays and Poems 141
    Videos, Storytelling, Art and Interactive Media 150
    Books or Magazines with a Powers Quilt on the Cover 152
    Inspired Quilts 153

TIMELINE 156

FURTHER AREAS FOR EXPLORATIONS 170

ABOUT THE AUTHOR 177

Acknowledgments

Researching African American quilt history is absolutely *fun*! And stitching together this book has been its own adventure. I had no idea when I started to compile a simple annotated bibliography of references to Harriet Powers that I would eventually travel beyond the Library of Congress to Athens, Georgia, Boston, Massachusetts, Westerly, Rhode Island, or even to the actual house where Harriet Powers' *Pictorial Quilt* once hung on one of the walls.

I also had no idea, when I started, of all the gracious assistance I would receive on this adventure. I am particularly thankful to Doris Bowman, Associate Curator at the Smithsonian National Museum of American History, and Susan Ward, Research Fellow at the Museum of Fine Arts, Boston. Each of these women patiently answered my many detailed questions about Harriet Powers and her quilts.

I am also grateful to the extraordinary kindness of Mrs. Katharine Hall Preston, granddaughter of Dr. Charles C. Hall, the 1898 recipient of Harriet Powers' *Pictorial Quilt*. Mrs. Preston and her husband, John, opened their home to me and shared intimate family stories about Dr. Hall, Rev. Basil Hall, and the *Pictorial Quilt*. I am also thankful to Mr. Robert Utter, Mr. Adolph Cavallo, and Mr. Carl Zahn for sharing their personal memories of the *Pictorial Quilt*.

Several lovely people assisted me at helpful or unexpected points in my research: Kentucky quilter Karen Davis; Virginia Eisemon at the Smithsonian Institution; Antoine James, archives technician at the Robert W. Woodruff Library at the Atlanta University Center; Jane Maxson, volunteer at the Westerly Public Library in Westerly, Rhode Island; author Gerald Hausman; and Electra Yourke (for a delightful conversation). And, at the very last days before this book was sent to be printed, Peter Drummey, Elaine Grublin, and Tracy Potter of the Massachusetts Historical Society graciously and quickly searched a few files for me and found three previously unrecognized treasures from 1961.

In Athens, a host of folks provided research assistance for which I'm most appreciative. They include historian Dr. Al Hester; Laura W. Carter, Heritage Room Librarian, and Carrie Ann Mumah, PR specialist, at the

Athens-Clarke County Library in Athens, Georgia; Mary Linnemann at the Hargrett Rare Book & Manuscript Library at the University of Georgia; photography historian Dr. W. Robert Nix; researcher Amy Sanders; historian Charlotte Marshall; and Nona Thornton, President of the Clarke-Oconee Genealogical Society (for passing along an email I sent and opening a world of Athens historians to me).

Who would have guessed a citizen of an Iowa town called Keokuk would play a role in Harriet Powers' story? I am thankful Leah Gudgel, Trustee of the Lorene Curtis Diver Memorial Trust, took my unexpected phone call on New Year's Eve 2008. I am very grateful for the generous assistance of time, effort, and hospitality Julie O'Connor of the Lee County Historical Society in Keokuk gave to me. Her February 2009 email with her discovery of a long-forgotten, nineteenth-century correspondence and photographic stash nearly caused me to scream aloud during a work-related conference (yes, I know, shouldn't open personal email during office hours!). I also appreciate the kindness and patient assistance of Tonya Boltz of the Keokuk Public Library.

I thank my friend Dr. Carolyn Mazloomi for her steadfast support and for listening to my "why" and "what if" questions and to my constant updates as tiny seeds in this research were planted, emerged, and bloomed in ways no one could have foreseen.

Finally, I appreciate my young cousin Astrid Hacker for her typing assistance, Brenda Grady for her insightful comments about the early drafts, and my dear Mom, Elizabeth A. Hicks, who has read and commented on this book at least a half-dozen times.

My only regret with this research is that Cuesta Benberry (1923 – 2007), my quilt history mentor, was not here to share in it. She would have *loved* this adventure!

I have diligently tried to ensure the accuracy of the bibliographic listings and historical narratives within these pages and accept responsibility for any mistakes. In the years and decades to come others will write about Harriet Powers and her quilts. I hope the pages here will be of assistance.

Kyra E. Hicks, f.w.c.
Arlington, Virginia

Foreword

Among the many titles held by Kyra E. Hicks, her latest journey into the history of African American quilting has earned her yet another— *Free Woman of Color—or FWC*. In *This I Accomplish*, we are once again treated to her sublime ability to combine audacity with humility as a scholar. Kyra had the audacity, guided by her humility, to ask the questions that produced this book—she asked what she *didn't know* as opposed to what she knew about Harriet Powers and the brilliance of her spirit-driven quilts. *This I Accomplish* is the work of a truly free woman—free from the academy, free from the assumptions of a traditional academic, free from the need to know-it-all, free from being in her own way, free from the fear of posing a basic question—what did/do African Americans think, know, feel, experience, and see in the world?

If more scholars posed research questions with the understanding that African Americans think, know, feel, experience, and see—this book would have been written before now. We would know what this book tells us about Harriet Powers and the America she lived in before now. But too few scholars pose such questions about Black women and quilts. This is why Kyra Hicks, as a *Free Woman of Color* with audacity, humility, and respect for Harriet's powers, researched and wrote *This I Accomplish*—and they didn't.

This I Accomplish is a book that will challenge many assumptions about this piece of American material culture as well as about the quilter herself. Like Kyra Hicks, Harriet Powers was a *Free Woman of Color*. It takes one to know one, which is one more reason that this book is in your hands.

There is so much more I could say. But I'm getting out of the way so that you can read *This I Accomplish* and say it yourself—to as many people as you can.

Bill Gaskins
Department of Art & Design Theory & History
Parsons The New School for Design

Introduction

Harriet Powers' quilts still fascinate us nearly 125 years after she stitched them. How and why did her two known surviving pieces, the *Bible Quilt* and the *Pictorial Quilt*, end up at major U.S. museums? What does the literature say about this noted quilter and her memorable works?

This I Accomplish: Harriet Powers' Bible Quilt and Other Pieces tries to address these questions by combining both rigorous research methodology and old fashion storytelling based on verifiable truths.

I first started writing this book as a simple annotative bibliography. Then I started to notice that some researchers would make statements about Harriet Powers or her quilts without citing any verifiable references. The more I noticed this, the "curiouser and curiouser" I became. My curiosity grew into a personal game to challenge much of what I read about Harriet Powers and her quilts—to challenge assumptions and conjectures.

This I Accomplish: Harriet Powers' Bible Quilt and Other Pieces brings to light new, exciting facts—many never before published:

- Complete exhibition history for both known Powers quilts
- Proof Harriet Powers was a literate, award-winning quilter who stitched at least five quilts and promoted her own quiltmaking skills
- Name of a potential second buyer of the *Bible Quilt*. No, Jennie Smith wasn't the only person who actively sought to own the quilt!
- Name of another Black woman artist Jennie Smith collected
- Actual contents of Jennie Smith's will
- Profiles of the three men who once owned the *Pictorial Quilt*
- Unveiling of a young artist who added to the *Pictorial Quilt*
- Proof the *Pictorial Quilt* was nearly removed from purchase consideration in 1961 in favor of continued ownership in a private family collection
- Price offered and accepted for the *Pictorial Quilt* in 1961
- Name of the person who first made the connection in the twentieth century that Harriet Powers stitched both the *Bible Quilt* and the *Pictorial Quilt*

This I Accomplish: Harriet Powers' Bible Quilt and Other Pieces is primarily for those, whether layperson or academic, interested in this marvelous quilter. It will also appeal to quilt and art historians and, maybe, a museum curator or two. I hope this book adds to local Athens, Georgia history, particularly that of the African American community.

This book can be read like a patchwork quilt—out of sequence, in small pieces, or gobbled whole in chapter order. There are more than 200 footnotes and a link to an interactive map to encourage further research on Powers and her quilts.

I tried to make this book accessible. At times, I insert myself in the narrative to speak directly to you, the reader. I can't help it—this research was so much fun! Let me tell you, it was very hard to keep secret the new, verifiable discoveries as they were uncovered. Many times I felt like a Clio Browne, a Tamara Hayle, or a Marti MacAlister, each a fictional African American female detective, on a quest to solve an impossible mystery. Many times I wanted badly to share the latest research tidbit with you on Black Threads (www.BlackThreads.blogspot.com), my African American quilt history blog. The adventure was so exhilarating!

There are still mysteries to Powers' story that I have not been able to solve, such as how much the *Pictorial Quilt* was purchased for in 1898 or whether any additional, physical quilts by Powers still exist.

Through the years, some writers have attributed various theories to Powers' artwork. For the record, I have found no primary or secondary nineteenth-century evidence whatsoever that Harriet Powers stitched any codes, directions, or other Underground Railroad quilted map nonsense into either the *Bible Quilt* or the *Pictorial Quilt*. I don't believe she did.

Over the decades, the Powers' quilts have been called by different names. For clarity, I refer to her quilt at the Smithsonian National Museum of American History as the *Bible Quilt* and her piece at the Museum of Fine Arts, Boston as the *Pictorial Quilt*.

Based on at least three records, Powers' first name was actually spelled Harriett. I use the present-day spelling of her name in this book.

I invite you to enjoy *This I Accomplish: Harriet Powers' Bible Quilt and Other Pieces*.

The Bible Quilt

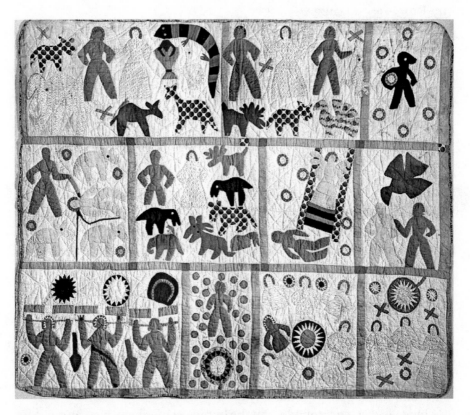

Bible Quilt by **Harriet Powers**. c. 1885-1886. All cotton, pieced and appliquéd. 75 X 89-3/8 inches. Smithsonian Institution, National Museum of American History, Washington, D.C. Gift of Mr. and Mrs. H. M. Heckman. T.14713.

Quilt Block Descriptions

Today, the *Bible Quilt* is housed at the Smithsonian National Museum of American History in Washington, D.C. Jennie Smith, who purchased the quilt from Harriet Powers, recorded from Powers' own descriptions what each block meant. The eleven blocks of the quilt can be described as follows:

Top Row – left to right
1. Adam and Eve naming the animals, including a camel, elephant, leviathan, and ostrich, in the Garden of Eden. Adam and Eve are also being tempted by a crawling serpent.
2. Adam and Eve with their son, Cain. A bird of paradise, made of red and green calico, is stitched in the bottom right corner.
3. The Devil with pink eyes stands surrounded by seven stars.

Middle Row – left to right
4. Cain killing his brother Abel, who is lying in a stream of his own blood. The sheep Cain is tending witness the attack.
5. Cain and his wife in the City of Nod. An orange calico lion stands among bears, an elk, leopards, and a "kangaroo hog."
6. Jacob sleeps while a winged angel seems to ascend or descend Jacob's ladder.
7. A dove from heaven flying over Jesus and John the Baptist after John baptized the Son of God.

Bottom Row – left to right
8. A bleeding Jesus crucified with two thieves. The circular objects above the crosses "represent the darkness over the earth and the moon turning into blood."
9. Judas Iscariot surrounded by thirty pieces of silver, his payment for betraying Jesus. The pieces of silver were originally made of green calico fabric. The largest circular object is a star "that appeared in 1886 for the first time in three hundred years."
10. Christ with his disciples at the Last Supper. According to Jennie Smith's letter sharing Powers' own description, it is Judas Iscariot who is "clothed in drab, being a little off-color in character."
11. The Holy Family, Mary, Joseph, and Jesus, with the Star of Bethlehem shining over them. The crosses represent the burden Christ carried in life.

Exhibition History

Countless numbers of people have seen the *Bible Quilt* on display over the last one hundred years, especially as it had been on display at the Smithsonian for more than thirty, almost continuous, years. Special thanks to Doris Bowman, Associate Curator, Division of Home and Community Life, Smithsonian National Museum of American History, for her assistance in compiling this exhibition history of the *Bible Quilt* since 1886.

Date	Exhibit
1886	Cotton Fair, Athens, Georgia. Most likely this was the Northeast Georgia Fair held Nov 9 – 13.
Sept. 18 – Dec. 31, 1895	Cotton States and International Exposition in Atlanta, Georgia. The *Bible Quilt* is on display in the Negro Building.
Apr. 1969 – 1975	Smithsonian National Museum of History and Technology, Washington, D.C. on display on the first floor near the Foucault Pendulum.
June 1976 – Feb. 27, 1991	Smithsonian National Museum of History and Technology, Washington, DC on display in the exhibit "A Nation of Nations," the museum's bicentennial exhibit. The museum's name was changed in 1980 to the National Museum of American History.
Apr. 23, 1991 – Apr. 10, 2002	Smithsonian National Museum of American History, Washington, D.C. on display in the remodeled exhibit "Life in America – After the Revolution."
Nov. 17, 2006 – Apr.13, 2008	Smithsonian National Air & Space Museum, Washington, D.C. on display in the exhibit "Treasures of American History" as part of the Expressions of Faith section. You can see the *Bible Quilt* on display by watching this You

Tube video: "Harriet Powers' Bible Quilt at the Air & Space Museum in DC." www.youtube.com/watch?v=WZKwP7W9Op8

The *Bible Quilt* is now in the National Museum of American History Textile Collection's storage room. You can request to see the *Bible Quilt* by appointment with the Division of Textiles or during the museum's "Behind the Scenes" tour by appointment on the second and fourth Tuesdays of the month. Visit the museum's website at: http://americanhistory.si.edu or contact the museum directly at:

National Museum of American History
Smithsonian Institution
P.O. Box 37012, Textiles Collection, MRC 617
Washington, DC 20013-7012
Phone (202) 633-3794

Quilt Exhibit, Interior of Negro Building, Atlanta Exposition.

The *Bible Quilt* on exhibit at the 1895 Cotton States and International Exposition, Atlanta, GA. Photograph courtesy of the Littleton Public Library, B. W. Kilburn Stereoview Collection, #10688, Littleton, NH.

Typically, the story of the *Bible Quilt* includes references to its maker, Harriet Powers; Jennie Smith, who purchased the quilt; and Harold Heckman, the executor of Smith's estate. The narrative is seemingly so well-known by quilt historians that I had no intentions of repeating it in what I thought would be an annotative bibliography about Harriet Powers and her quilts. But while compiling the bibliography, I started asking myself a few questions and challenging the assumptions to the story about the *Bible Quilt*.

The first question I remember asking myself was "What was the date of the Cotton Fair where Jennie Smith said she first saw the *Bible Quilt*?" Look at the literature. Every reference says the Cotton Fair in Athens, Georgia took place in 1886. But none has ever published the dates of the fair. To my utter delight, locating the dates led to learning about another 1886 Athens fair and the noteworthy African American-made quilts displayed there.

My curiosity went next to the contents of the Jennie Smith Papers held at the Hargrett Rare Book & Manuscript Library at the University of Georgia. What the heck was inside the Papers? In compiling the annotative bibliography, I hadn't seen anyone reference the Papers. Why not? Was any additional information about Smith's relationship with Powers located there? I spent a day reviewing the items. Among the five boxes of notes, letters, scrapbooks, newspapers, photographs, and artwork by Jennie Smith, I found one or two gems!

Again challenging the narrative of the *Bible Quilt* story, I wondered just how the quilt really came to be at the Smithsonian. Popular lore is that Jennie Smith didn't mention the quilt in her will and that her executor, Harold Heckman, later decided to give the quilt to the nation's museum. While compiling the annotative bibliography, I noticed no one actually cited Smith's will. Why not? As quilt historians, do we really know what Smith's last written wishes were or do we just assume? My hands shook and I screamed when I read Smith's will. "Oh my God!" was all I could repeat.

On Monday, December 29, 2008, I took a vacation day from work and visited the National Museum of American History to review its files on the *Bible Quilt*. I wanted to double check my bibliographic references. On this visit, the Textile Department staff shared a faded photograph of the *Bible Quilt* with notes from a woman in Keokuk, Iowa who wanted to purchase the *Bible Quilt*. I had never seen or read about this faded picture. Who was this woman? Why was she interested in the *Bible Quilt*? I spent the next eight or nine weeks corresponding with anyone in Keokuk who would answer my emails and phone calls. I even corresponded with a lovely Keokuk historian who sold Keokuk-related postcards on eBay. I searched for articles about the woman in the Library of Congress.

Finally, I wrote a profile of the woman, who died in 1922, for this book. But, I wanted a photograph of her to complete the profile. Could someone in Keokuk help me locate one? Little did I realize how critical my absurd insistence on locating a photograph of this woman would be.

In late February 2009, Julie O'Connor of the Lee County Historical Society sent me an email letting me know that she discovered a long-forgotten Historical Society folder with a photograph of the woman and other assorted nineteenth-century correspondence about a certain quilt. On March 5, 2009, I came home from work to find a FedEx envelope from Mrs. O'Connor at my front door. Not wanting to be an eager beaver, I read the day's *Washington Post* and ate dinner before opening the packet.

After coffee, I ripped open the FedEx envelope. I sifted through the photocopies in amazement. Then my eyes landed on an elegantly handwritten name that caused me to scream and immediately cry—puffy red eyes, snotty nose, guttural cry. I couldn't stop my hands from shaking as I dialed my friend, curator Dr. Carolyn Mazloomi, at home. She thought I had suffered another death in the family as I couldn't stop crying. Finally, I was able to tell her, between hiccups, what I held in my hand. I won't share the profanity she exclaimed over and over.

I once visited the Smithsonian Institution and privately saw Harriet Powers' *Bible Quilt* in person as it lay in storage. I so wanted to touch the quilt, but I was afraid there might be security cameras around and sirens would go off. I was mere inches from the fabrics Harriet Powers touched.

In the following pages, I'd like to share with you the story of the *Bible Quilt* in a new way by introducing you to six people who have actually, or possibly, touched the quilt before it arrived forty years ago via the United States Postal Service to the Smithsonian Institution.

Jennie Smith (1862—1946)

Jennie Smith, who purchased Harriet Powers' *Bible Quilt*, was born in Athens, Georgia on April 24, 1862 to Susan Harris (1838—1921) of Meriwether County, Georgia and Wales Smith (1824—1870), a cotton buyer from New England. Smith had two siblings. Her sister, Ida, died in childhood. Her brother, Wales Wynton Smith, became a noted journalist.

Smith attended and graduated from the Lucy Cobb Institute, a private school for Southern girls in Athens. She studied art at the Institute as well as in Baltimore, New York, and Paris.[1] She began her teaching career as art professor at the Lucy Cobb Institute upon her graduation in 1880.[2] She was nineteen years old.

Today, we know from Jennie Smith's own handwriting that she first saw Harriet Powers' *Bible Quilt* at the "Cotton Fair of 1886," which included a Wild West show, a circus, and two cotton weddings.[3] One question quilt historians have not yet answered is the date range of the Cotton Fair held in Athens, Georgia. Was the fair officially called the "Cotton Fair" or was that just a popular local name? In January 2009, I spent a day reviewing microfilm from January 1 to December 31, 1886 from the *Weekly Banner-Watchman*, the local Athens newspaper. I did not find a single article about a Cotton Fair, a circus or Wild West show. Does this mean there was no Cotton Fair?

No, it doesn't. With blurry eyes, I could have missed a reference. Or, perhaps the local paper did not report on the Cotton Fair, which I doubt. Or, Jennie Smith could have been mistaken about the year, which I also doubt as 1886 would be a significant year for her. Or, the Cotton Fair could have been the local, popular name for the more formal Northeast Georgia Fair.

A year earlier in 1885, the Northeast Georgia Fair was first held in Athens from November 4 - 6. Fair activities included horse racing,

---

[1] Bessie Mell Lane, "Miss Jennie Smith and Lucy Cobb." In Higher Education for Women in the South: A History of Lucy Cobb Institute 1858 – 1994 (Athens, GA: Georgia Southern Press, 1994), 273 – 275.

[2] Phinizy Spalding, ed., Higher Education for Women in the South: A History of Lucy Cobb Institute 1858 – 1994 (Athens, GA: Georgia Southern Press, 1994), 44.

[3] Jennie Smith, "A Biblical Quilt," Handwritten, nine-page essay, not dated, Textile Department, Smithsonian National Museum of American History, Washington, D.C.

livestock exhibitions, baseball games, foodstuffs, and craft judging. According to one newspaper report, fair organizers created a Ladies Department and "spared no effort to induce the ladies to take an interest in the fair."[4] Five thousand people attended the fair's opening day.[5] The Lucy Cobb Institute exhibited drawings and paintings at this event.[6]

In 1886, Athens cotton farmers experienced a record yield. One cotton merchant made front page headlines by declaring 62,000 bales of cotton at season's end, up 15 percent over the previous year.[7]

The second annual Northeast Georgia Fair was held in Athens November 9 – 13, 1886. Secretary W. D. Griffeth and Assistant Secretary W. S. Morris received and documented each fair entry in an official records book. Activities again included daily horse racing, a cattle show, poultry and crop displays (including cotton bales and seeds), art, craft and foodstuff exhibits. Fair Association President W. B. Thomas pointed out to one reporter, "As you see, every inch of space is packed, and there is scarcely room to walk around. Both our merchants and farmers have taken great interest in the fair, while the ladies have surpassed themselves."[8]

The *Banner-Watchman* newspaper noted the varied activities by women at the Fair:

"A B-W editor yesterday undertook the Herculean task of invading the ladies' department and writing up the display but he almost gave up in despair. The large room is literally packed with the most beautiful goods, every article well deserving special mention, but to do even partial justice to all the exhibits would require a volume as extensive as an encyclopedia. Through the kindness of Mrs. Morris we were enabled to secure a partial list of the exhibits. It was impossible to learn the names of all the exhibitors, as they are only entered by numbers, and it would be like searching for a needle in a hay-stack to go through the

---

4 "The Northeast Georgia Fair," Atlanta Constitution, Oct. 19, 1885, p. 2.

5 "The Northeast Georgia Fair," Atlanta Constitution, Nov. 6, 1885, p. 2.

6 "The Northeast Georgia Fair," Atlanta Constitution, Nov. 7, 1885, p. 2.

7 "Over Sixty Thousand. Close of the Cotton Season Yesterday," Weekly Banner-Watchman (Athens, GA), Sept. 7, 1886, p. 1.

8 "The Fair!," Weekly Banner-Watchman (Athens, GA), Nov. 16, 1886, p. 1. Oh, that an ambitious researcher could determine whether the Secretary's record books still exists!

hundreds of entries on the Secretaries' books. The ceiling is draped with quilts, counterpanes, afghans, knit work, etc. etc., while show-cases that line the long counters are filled with finer articles. We never saw such a display of rich quilts and do not envy the committee their task of making a selection to award the premiums."[9]

The Fair displayed many, many quilts! There were at least twenty-two entries for calico quilts alone.[10] Other quilts showcased included a silk patched quilt, a crocheted quilt, a log cabin quilt, and multiple crazy and cradle quilts. More than twenty-five quilters were individually named in various newspaper articles.

Jules Cohen, a local merchant who sold "beautiful fabrics" and later became the first Jewish elected public official in Athens, advertised heavily in the *Banner-Watchman* newspaper and declared himself the "Leader in Dry Goods, Dictator of Fashions, and Regulator of Price."[11] At the Fair, Cohen awarded a $5 prize to Mrs. F. W. Lucas for the best crazy quilt.[12]

Harriet Powers' name was not listed in any of the newspaper accounts I read.

Did the Northeast Georgia Fair even allow entries from African Americans? Presumably yes, if this is the Fair where Jennie Smith saw Harriet Powers' *Bible Quilt* on display.

Was the Northeast Georgia Fair segregated? Specifically, was there a separate area for displays by African Americans? In many fairs, African American exhibits were shown in a separate building, sometimes referred to as the "Negro Building." I didn't read any articles that hinted at a segregated display, although there could have been one not reported in the local newspaper.

---

[9] "The Fair!," Weekly Banner-Watchman (Athens, GA), Nov. 11, 1886, p. 4. Though the article does not say, I suspect Mrs. Morris is the wife of W. S. Morris, a Fair secretary.

[10] "The Fair!," Daily Banner-Watchman (Athens, GA), Nov. 11, 1886, p. 1.

[11] Weekly Banner-Watchman (Athens, GA), Sept. 21, 1886 and Oct. 26, 1886. See also Steven S. Bush, "The Jewish Community in Athens, Georgia: The First Hundred Years," Athens Historian, vol. 7, Fall 2002, p. 1 – 8.

[12] "End of the Fair," Sunday Banner-Watchman (Athens, GA), Nov. 14, 1886, p. 1. According to MeasuringWorth.com, $5 in 1886 is worth $118.04 in 2008 dollars.

Black Americans didn't seem barred from the fair. Two newspaper articles mentioned African Americans specifically by calling attention to their ethnicity. One article recalled a "negro" who lost $8 on the fairground's softball field.[13] Another article promoted a "Negro Foot Race." The fair management anticipated many entries for this segregated race and offered a special prize for its winner.[14]

I suspect no African American exhibitor at the Northeast Georgia Fair was mentioned by name in local newspapers. This would include Harriet Powers. In 1886, there was no local Black community newspaper.[15] How fascinating it would have been to read news of the fair from a Black perspective.

Jennie Smith, now twenty-four years old, actively participated in the Northeast Georgia Fair of 1886. Her own watercolors were on display and won a prize. She also won a "special premium" for an art display.[16] Several of her art students exhibited charcoal drawings. One newspaper noted Smith's progressive (for the late nineteenth century!) teaching method. Her students created artwork not copied from existing masterpieces, but created from live models, a "method of teaching now in Northern schools."[17]

One newspaper devoted approximately seven column inches to describing Smith's expert and extensive contributions to the fair:

"The Banner-Watchman has already noticed at some length the art display at the fair, and has spoken in complimentary terms of the exhibition of pictures, china painting, etc., and of the exhibitors. The mind that conceived, and the hand that arranged all this has not yet received the reward that its untiring energy and unmistakable talent deserves. Perhaps, in the whole city of Athens, there is no young lady who has so decided a talent for painting and etching as Miss Jennie Smith. There is hardly a home where decorative art is admired and appreciated that has not some

13 "The Fair," Banner-Watchman (Athens, GA), Nov. 11, 1886, p. 4.

14 "A Negro Foot Race," Weekly Banner-Watchman (Athens, GA), Nov. 16, 1886.

15 The Athens Clipper, a local African American four-page newspaper edited by S. B. Davis, started in 1887. It is unclear if physical copies or microfilm of the newspaper still exists. For more information on African American newspapers published in Athens, read "The Black Journalists" in A Story Untold: Black Men and Women in Athens History by Michael L. Thurmond.

16 "End of the Fair," Sunday Banner-Watchman (Athens, GA), Nov. 14, 1886, p. 1.

17 "The Fair!," Weekly Banner-Watchman (Athens, GA), Nov. 11, 1886, p. 1.

specimen of this young lady's skill. Miss Smith loves her work with all the enthusiasm of youth, and her handiwork is rendered all the more attractive as it is the result of a cultured and strikingly original mind. The exhibition at the fair contained many of her exquisite specimens of painting, but with a modesty characteristic of real genius, she placed her work in the back ground and that of her pupils in the most conspicuous place. Miss Smith received her artistic training in Athens. She rapidly acquired a degree of skill in her profession that was as remarkable as it was gratifying. China painting, plaque painting, panel painting, etching, and the art in all of its branches was soon mastered by her, and then to get further assistance and to obtain access to a richer range of subjects, Miss Smith passed several winters in Baltimore pursuing her favorite work. For some time past she has been engaged instructing a class of young ladies. That she has been a diligent and successful teacher is demonstrated by the beautiful and elaborate display of art at the fair grounds, and that she is proud of her pupils is illustrated by the conspicuous positions their work occupy. The many friends of Miss Smith in compliment to her gathered together as many of her beautiful specimens as the short time allowed them, and placed them on exhibition. The fair regulations require all exhibitors to be nameless, but if the looker on would have been told the artist of many beautiful conceptions admired during the week, he or she would have been amazed at the fertility of Miss Smith's genius and the rapidity that she executed her work. This young lady so popular and admired by our people for her many excellent traits and talents has a pleasant vein of humor; some of her most admired works are humorous in their character, and attract by their quaintness of conception as well as by their brilliant execution. It is not a prediction, but a reality as far as future events can become real, that Miss Smith is destined to occupy no inconsiderable place in her chosen profession."[18]

What a remarkable week Jennie Smith experienced attending and participating in the Northeast Georgia Fair. She likely spent one day with her art students walking the aisles and comparing their creations to others on display. She likely spent another day accompanying her mother, Susan

---

[18] "A Talented Young Artist," Weekly Banner-Watchman, Nov. 16, 1886, page unclear.

Harris Smith, who was forty-eight years old, to the fair. How proud her mother must have been to read the glowing *Banner-Watchman* article about her daughter.

Neither mother nor daughter could imagine the tragedy to come one week later.

Jennie Smith's brother, Wales Wynton Smith, an "energetic" journalist who legally changed his name to Wales Wynton, lived in Birmingham, Alabama. Early in his career he was an Athens correspondent for the *Atlanta Constitution*, then manager for the paper in its Macon, Georgia office.[19] Later he was city editor of the *Daily Age* in Birmingham when a bout with typhoid fever forced him to leave that job. Once he recovered months later, he became city editor of the *Evening Chronicle* in Birmingham.

On Friday, November 12, 1886, Wynton met with a friend, who was also a fellow reporter, for about an hour. Wynton shared with his friend that a new opportunity had appeared and he was leaving the newspaper profession. Wynton, who was only thirty years old, excused himself, saying he had not felt well all day and was going home to rest.[20]

Wynton's sickness became grave and his mother was summoned from Athens by telegram to be with him. She arrived by train on Thursday, November 18.[21] By now Wynton could no longer speak and slipped in and out of consciousness. By Saturday at noon, Susan Smith telegraphed her daughter, Jennie, that she "had no hopes of his recovery."[22] His mother was "with him when he died," on Saturday evening, November 20, a week after his sister's glorious triumph at the Northeast Georgia Fair.[23]

Many friends and fellow reporters accompanied Wales Wynton's body back to Athens, where he was taken from the train station directly to

---

[19] While in Macon, Wynton was mistakenly thought to be involved in a letter published by the Cincinnati *Enquirer* by "Sherwood," a man later identified as Frederick S. Brown. Wynton's life was threatened. He left town immediately and hid in the mountains of Tennessee and in a small Mexican town for several weeks. When he finally returned home to Athens, he gave an interview with the local paper. See "Wynton's Woes," Banner-Watchman (Athens, GA), Jan. 19, 1886, p. 1. See also "Indignant Macon Citizens," New York Times, Feb. 28, 1885, p. 1.

[20] "Wales Wynton," Atlanta Constitution, Nov. 22, 1886, p. 7.

[21] "Wales Wynton Dying," Atlanta Constitution, Nov. 19, 1886, p. 1.

[22] "Wales Wynton Dead," Weekly Banner-Watchman, Nov. 23, 1886, p. 1.

[23] "Death of Wales Wynton," Atlanta Constitution, Nov. 21, 1886, p. 6.

the Oconee Hill Cemetery for burial in the family's plot. His mother, was too overcome with grief to attend the ceremony.[24]

Annual Athens Colored Fairs

On Monday, November 22, 1886, the first annual Colored Fair opened on the same Athens fairgrounds as the Northeast Georgia Fair. The organizers of the Colored Fair included Madison Davis, president; Wesley Williams, vice-president; John Mack, treasurer; and E. W. Brydie, W. H. Easlis, and R. S. Harris, secretaries.[25]

Augusta, Georgia lawyer Judson W. Lyons gave the opening day remarks. He would later be appointed Register of the U.S. Treasury (1898 – 1906) and his signature would be printed on all U.S. paper currencies during his tenure.

One local newspaper devoted twenty-two column inches to details about the Colored Fair, including the noteworthy quilts and other needlearts created by Black women from Athens and surrounding communities:

"Yesterday morning the Banner-Watchman sent a special reporter to the colored fair, to see what progress these people had made...

"The housekeepers' department was well filled, and we noticed specimens of wines, jellies, preserves, pickles, etc., that were highly creditable...

"The women's department is well filled and highly creditable... There are a great many very pretty quilts and home-made bed coverings. We noticed especially quilts exhibited by Caroline Thomas, Mary Biniard, Phillis Elder, and others. Mary Biniard has a white knit quilt that is quite pretty. There is some nice fancy work, conspicuous among which we noticed silk pillows and cushions by Pinkie Davis, Lucy Brown, Cordelia Lewis, Ella Davis, Maria Cole and Lizzie Climons... There was also a very pretty rug, made of scraps, a homespun pieced quilt

---

[24] Weekly Banner-Watchman, Nov. 30, 1886.

[25] "Affairs About Athens," Atlanta Constitution, Aug. 21, 1886, p. 2. Madison Davis, the Colored Fair President, was also elected to the Georgia State Legislature during Reconstruction and appointed as postmaster for Athens, GA (1882 – 1886 and 1890 – 1893).

and pretty pillow shams, of every design. Phillis Brown exhibits a pair of cotton pillow shames, Berta White a pretty work basket made of shucks, and Emma Myrick embroidery. Precilla Heard has a dress and shirt made by her own hands, and Phillis Stubbs a quilt with 1,000 pieces...

"Taken altogether, the fair is decidedly creditable, and it deserves encouragement. The weather is against the management, and if only a day or so of sunshine appears, the exhibition will be a financial success. Today some fine races will take place. The best of order is observed on the ground, and the officers do all in their power to make the fair successful. Exhibitions still continue to come in, and yesterday a large box was received from the Spelman Baptist College in Atlanta, containing some creditable specimens of crayon work, embroidery and sewing done by the pupils."[26]

As this article demonstrates, Black women in Athens were quilting and exhibiting their art in the late nineteenth century. At the time, no gallery or museum system was open to Black women artists. Local fairs were an acceptable and popular display avenue.

The annual Athens Colored Fair lasted at least through 1903, based on newspaper accounts. More research is needed on the Colored Fairs to gain deeper insights on quiltmaking in Athens during this time and to place Harriet Powers' quiltmaking and her quilt designs in the context of her community. For example, stitching a quilt with a Bible theme may not have been unusual in the late 1880s. At the 1886 Northeast Georgia Fair, one newspaper reported a crazy quilt "with an animal embroidered very daintily in each square. One naturally thinks of Noah's ark when he sees an elephant, giraffe, camel, lion, dog, cat, &c., all perfectly outlined and colored with the needle."[27] The following year at the Athens Colored Fair, the local newspaper reported that "[q]uilts, hand-made, of all descriptions, show a great deal of ingenuity, also a very large one, representing the crucifix; ... always has a large crowd around it."[28]

---

[26] "The Colored Fair," Weekly Banner-Watchman, Nov. 30, 1886, p. 1. Madison Davis, President of the Athens Colored Fair, was married to an Ella Davis. It's unclear if, though very likely, the Ella Davis listed in the article was Madison Davis' wife. According to U.S. Census data, Pinkie Davis, also in the article, was married, a seamstress, and resident of Athens.

[27] "The Fair!," Banner-Watchman (Athens, GA), Nov. 11, 1886, p. 4.

[28] "The Colored Fair," Weekly Banner-Watchman (Athens, GA), Nov. 15, 1887, p. 1.

Did Harriet Powers exhibit the *Bible Quilt*, which included a block featuring the Crucifixion, at the Athens Colored Fair? Did she attend the Fair with her family? How did she feel seeing the quilts on display at the Fair? Did she compare the designs to her own quiltmaking?

The *Weekly Banner-Watchman* mentioned a quilt with 1,000 pieces that Phillis Stubbs stitched and displayed at the Colored Fair of 1886. How common was it to count the number of pieces in a quilt in the 1880s? Was there competition among quilters for the highest number of pieces? How would such a 1,000 piece quilt compare to what we know today as scrap, postage stamp, or charm quilts? Were such numbered quilt patterns popular in Georgia during the 1880s?

Did African American quilters in Athens anticipate selling their quilts at local fairs? This is an interesting question. Of the Colored Fair, a local newspaper reporter wrote: "Several very pretty crazy quilts are on exhibition. These quilts are prettily finished off and if sold we daresay there will be some lively bidding among the white people."[29]

We do know that Jennie Smith, then twenty-eight years old, first saw Harriet Powers' *Bible Quilt* at the Cotton Fair, most likely the Northeast Georgia Fair, of 1886. The quilt's exposure at the Cotton Fair did eventually lead to a sale. Smith wrote about the transaction:

"… in one corner there hung a quilt which "captured my eye" and after much difficulty I found the owner, a negro woman who lives in the country on a little farm whereon she and her husband make a respectable living.

"She is about sixty five years old, of a burnt-ginger cake color, and is a very clean and interesting woman, who loves to talk of her "ole miss" and her life "'fo de war."

"The scenes on the quilt were biblical and I was fascinated.

"I offered to buy it, but it was not for sale at any price. After four years Harriet sent me word that I could buy it, if I wanted it.

"Alas! my financial affairs were at a low ebb and I could not purchase.

"Last year I sent her word I would buy it if she still wanted to dispose of it.

[29] "The Colored Fair," Weekly Banner-Watchman (Athens, GA), Nov. 15, 1887, p. 1.

"She arrived one afternoon in front of my door in an ox-cart, with the precious burden in her lap encased in a clean flour sack, which was still further enveloped in a crocus sack.

"She offered it for ten dollars, but I only had five to give.

"After going out and consulting her husband, she returned and said "'ownin ter de hardness of de times, my ole man 'lows I'd better teck hit," and not being a new woman, she obeyed.

"After giving me a full description of each scene with great earnestness, and deep piety she departed, but has been back several times to visit the darling offspring of her brain. She was only in a measure consoled for its loss when I promised to save her all my scraps."[30]

Cotton States and International Exposition 1895

The Cotton States and International Exposition was held from September 18 to December 31, 1895 in Atlanta, Georgia. Nearly 800,000 adults and children paid for admission to the Expo.[31]

Jennie Smith organized the display of her students' artwork in an exhibit at the Exposition in the Women's Building's Lucy Cobb Institute Room.[32] The contents of the room "attracted much attention."[33] Smith also arranged for the *Bible Quilt,* which she now owned, to be displayed in the segregated Negro Building so others could admire its beauty.

The Negro Building, organized by Irvine Garland Penn, was a popular destination. According to one newspaper reporter:

"The Paris exposition had its Eiffel tower, the world's fair had its Ferris wheel, but Atlanta has its negro building… as a drawing card… The difference between those three attractions, however, is that when you went up to the top of the Eiffel tower or were taken up in the Ferris wheel you returned to the earth no better

[30] Jennie Smith, Handwritten essay, c. 1891, Textile Department, Smithsonian National Museum of American History, Washington, D.C. The purchasing power of $5 in 1891 is $122 in 2008 dollars according to MeasuringWorth.com.

[31] Walter Gerald Cooper, The Cotton States and International Exposition and South, Illustrated Including the Official History of the Exposition (Atlanta: Illustrator Co., 1896), pp. 87 – 88.

[32] Judy L. Larson, Three Southern World's Fairs, PhD Diss., Emory University, 1998, p. 427.

[33] Cooper, The Cotton States, p. 79. Includes photograph of the Lucy Cobb Institute Room.

physically and very little better, if any mentally. But not so when you visit the negro building at our exposition. You will return with the impression that the southern negro is making rapid progress in all lines of industry, science and art. Yes, you will come out of the building improved physically, mentally and spiritually."[34]

Several dignitaries made a point of visiting the Negro Building. Mississippi Governor John M. Stone (1830—1900) made an "unheralded and unaccompanied" visit to the Expo in October 1895. One reporter who learned of the governor's presence wrote, "He was much interested in the negro building. Walking slowly through until he came upon the display sent by the negroes from Mississippi, he paused a few minutes and asked a number of questions of the colored custodian."[35]

President Grover Cleveland (1837—1908) spent a day at the Expo. He reviewed troops from a stand outside the Government Building and gave a public speech. After a formal lunch, the only other official event was an afternoon tour of the Negro Building.[36] One reporter noted: "Here the President seemed to relax the official frigidity which he maintained during most of his tour. He was waited upon by Commissioner Penn and other colored leaders, who explained to him fully all points of interest. He asked many questions, showing that he regarded the negro building as perhaps the most important in a political sense on the grounds. The colored people were highly elated by the interest the President took in what they had to show him, and are tonight his most enthusiastic admirers."[37]

Booker T. Washington (1856—1915), head of the Tuskegee Institute, was one of the Exposition's opening day speakers and a tour guide to the President. Maybe as they strolled through the Negro Building, they admired Harriet Powers' *Bible Quilt*.[38] They were not the only admirers.

---

34 H. R. Butler, "What The Negro is Doing," Atlanta Constitution, Oct. 13, 1895, p. 3.

35 "Gov. Stone in Town," Atlanta Constitution, Oct. 23, 1895, p. 6.

36 "Presidential Programme," Atlanta Constitution, Oct. 23, 1895, p. 2. See also Harper's Weekly, Nov. 2, 1895, for a full-page engraving of the President being welcomed to the Negro Building.

37 "Grover at the Fair," Chicago (Tribune), Oct. 24, 1995, p. 1.

38 "Now for Grover," Atlanta Constitution, Oct. 19, 1895, p. 1. Interestingly, Washington was also acquainted with Dr. Charles C. Hall, who would later own Harriet Powers' *Pictorial Quilt*.

Clara R. Jemison (1869—1907)

Twenty-six year old Clara R. Jemison, assistant editor of the *Tuscaloosa Times* newspaper and wife of William Carlos Jemison, two-time mayor of Tuscaloosa, Alabama (1880—1890, 1894—1900) and owner of the *Tuscaloosa Times*, attended the Cotton States and International Exposition. She reported on fair activities, particularly those in the Negro Building.

Clara R. Jemison, May 1899
Alabama Department of Archives and History, Montgomery, AL

Jemison wrote about five different African American-made quilts on display in the building, including a silk quilt stitched from "at least 1,000 pieces" by a woman nearly seventy years old.

She shared that an exhibit tour guide asked each person, "Have you seen the Biblical quilt?" Jemison wrote, "It (the quilt) seems to be her especial pride and the admiration of all the colored visitors. It was made long ago by a poor, ignorant slave who could not read, and whose only knowledge of the Bible was the stories told her by others more fortunate." Jemison provided no evidence why she wrote as fact that Harriet Powers was poor, uneducated and illiterate.

Though Jemison did not say explicitly whether she touched the *Bible Quilt*, she did provide an extensive first-person description of Harriet Powers' covering:

"Each square represents one of these stories, and the result would be amusing if it were not curious as a study of the impressions of an unenlightened mind when told of things she cannot understand. The foundation is made of pink calico, and the figures are then stitched on. There is Satan amid the seven stars, Satan himself made of the blackest material that could be found. Jacob's dream is represented by an angel with wings strongly resembling the modern sleeve, on a wonderful ladder, with a figure lying at the foot. There is Cain when he went in the land of Nod to get him a wife, surrounded by numerous animals, and a card affixed imparts the information that "the yellow animal is a lion." The Last Supper is represented by several light figures and one dark, which is Judas. The Crucifixion, however, is the most curious of all; her idea of darkness over the earth being represented by two black balls hovering just over the three figures on the crosses."[39]

Jemison's article about the exhibits in the Negro Building was syndicated to other newspapers.[40] In later years, Jemison's writings appeared in publications as varied as *Ladies Home Journal*, the *New York Evening Post,* and *The Silent Worker*, where she interviewed Helen Keller. Jemison took over the management of the *Tuscaloosa Times* when her husband died in 1901. Later, she sold the newspaper and moved with her two young children, William and Margaret, for a time to Montgomery, Alabama; later they settled in New York. She passed away in 1907 at the age of thirty-eight.

Lorene Curtis Diver (1846—1922)

Lorene Diver, another visitor to the Negro Building in 1895, was so enamored with the *Bible Quilt* she tried to purchase it.

Lorene Curtis Diver was a young girl when her family moved to Keokuk, Iowa from Lima, Ohio. She remembered the specific date her family arrived to their new home, April 14, 1865, the day President Abraham Lincoln was assassinated. Her family tree included at least two

---

[39] Clara R. Jemison, "Exhibit of the Negroes," Chicago Daily, Nov. 24, 1895, p. 30.

[40] "The Colored Race at Atlanta," Broad Ax (Salt Lake City, Utah), Dec. 7, 1895, pp. 1, 4. This article does not include a byline, but it mirrors Jemison's "Exhibit of the Negroes" article. It would be interesting to see whether this article was also published in the *Tuscaloosa Times*.

prominent individuals. One was her father's brother, Samuel Ryan Curtis (1805–1866), who served as mayor of Keokuk (1856), U.S. Congressman (1857–1861), and as Major General in the U.S. Army during the Civil War.[41] The other prominent person was Elihu Yale (1649–1721), the first major benefactor and eventual namesake of Yale University. Both Lorene and Elihu were descendants of the Yale family in Wales.[42]

At age twenty-four, Lorene married James Brice Diver (1847— 1930), an engineer and bridge builder. The couple's home was located at 525 North Third Street in Keokuk. Chiseled on the steps leading to the front door of their home was its name, "Port Sunshine."[43] The couple had two children. Their first daughter, Lavinia Diver, was born in 1871, but died in infancy. Their second and last child was another daughter, Helen Curtis Diver, born Thanksgiving Day 1875.

In 1874, months before her daughter Helen was born, the Divers attended the 21st Annual Iowa State Fair held in town.[44] Lorene exhibited a "handsome" stand of flowers in Floral Hall.[45] More importantly, she was a quilter. That year the Fair awarded prizes in fourteen different quilt categories. She won second prize in the "best silk crib quilt" category.[46]

Diver was also an active and well-regarded citizen of her community. She was the charter member of several organizations including the Audubon Society of Iowa (1886), for which she was elected President for several years; the Keokuk Chapter of the Daughters of the American Revolution (1898), which she started in her own home; the Monday Music Club (1900); the Wednesday Reading Club (1895); and the

---

[41] Wikipedia contributors, "Samuel Curtis," Wikipedia.com (accessed Feb. 15, 2009).

[42] Winona Evans Reeves, The Blue Book of Iowa Women: A History of Contemporary Women (Mexico, MO: Press of the Missouri Print. and Pub. Co., 1914), p. 143. See also Tom Gardner, "Living in the District: Port Sunshine and the World of Lorene Curtis Diver," Keokuk Confluence, Autumn 2008, pp. 4 - 5.

[43] Raymond E. Garrison, Goodbye, My Keokuk Lady (Hamilton, IL: Hamilton Press, 1962), p. 88. The chapter "Good Morning, Mrs. Sunshine!" profiles Lorene Diver on pp. 88 – 93. Includes photo of Diver as a child with her parents. Her home, Port Sunshine, still stands today. The home is also described in Tales of Early Keokuk Homes by Raymond E. Garrison (Hamilton, IL: Hamilton Press, 1959), p. 119.

[44] The Fair was held in Keokuk in 1869 – 1870 and 1874 – 1875. Visit the Iowa State Fair web site at www.IowaStateFair.com and look under About Us.

[45] "The State Fair: A Star Exhibition," Daily Gate City (Keokuk, IA), Sept. 23, 1874.

[46] "The State Fair: Premiums Awarded," Daily Gate City (Keokuk, IA), Sept. 24, 1874. I assume one must have actually made the quilt to enter it. Thus, Lorene Diver was a quilter.

Keokuk Humane Society (1912).[47]

In 1891, the couple's fifteen-year-old daughter, Helen, died. At one point Lorene Diver shared, "I spent a number of years trying to ease over a great sorrow." To help overcome her grief, she turned toward the study of photography and found a passion. "Photography is not a profession, but a disease, like motoring and golf," she once said humorously.[48]

On September 18, 1895, the *Daily Gate City*, the local Keokuk newspaper, printed a front page story about the "Exposition At Atlanta."[49] Undoubtedly, Diver read the news account that hailed the Cotton States and International Exposition as "the greatest event in the history of the big show."

At some point, Diver, and presumably with her husband, James, traveled 740 miles from Keokuk to Atlanta to attend the exposition. Diver, who was forty-nine years old, packed her camera equipment to record the adventure. It was once noted that "[s]he had a genuine interest in the multitude of places and things she saw, and she studied them intently on the ground. She studied history and art and sociology."[50]

Lorene Diver spent time visiting and enjoying the artifacts at the exposition, including those in the Negro Building. There she spied the *Bible Quilt*. As a quilter herself, she would have appreciated the quilt's composition and craftsmanship. She must have touched the cotton fabrics Harriet Powers stitched as she sought to photograph the piece.

Diver eventually obtained permission to photograph the *Bible Quilt*. One can only imagine what kind of camera equipment she used in 1895. However, the lighting was not optimal and she felt the resulting photograph was not successful. As a result, she hired a local professional photographer to capture the quilt's image.

The professionally taken, sepia-colored photograph of the *Bible Quilt* measured 9" x 7.5" and was mounted on stiff cardboard about 10" x 12."

[47] "At Memory's Gate," the funeral program for Lorene Curtis Diver, June 7, 1922. A copy of the twenty-four page program is available from the Keokuk, Iowa Public Library. See also "Death of Mrs. J. B. Diver," Daily Gate City (Keokuk, IA), June 7, 1922, p. 9.

[48] Garrison, Goodbye, My Keokuk Lady, p. 91.

[49] The Daily Gate City (Keokuk, IA) Fair stories: Sept. 18, 19; Oct. 2, 15, 23, 1895.

[50] "At Memory's Gate," the funeral program for Lorene Curtis Diver, June 7, 1922.

At least two copies of the professional photograph survive today. One is owned by the Smithsonian and the other by the Lee County Historical Society in Keokuk.[51] There doesn't appear to be a stamp or other notation indicating which local photographer took the image.

Lorene Diver captured her impression of the quilt and her desire to purchase it in her own handwriting on the back of the photograph:

"A Sermon in Patchwork"

"[T]his quilt was made by Mrs. Harriet Powers in 1888—an aged colo[red] [w]oman & exhibited in the colored peoples building. Atlanta Cotton States Fair 1895. Her idea was that so many tributes were paid to stars, leaves & blossoms by taking them for quilt patterns that she would 'preach the gospel' in patch work—tell the story of the fall of Adam & Eve …

"Note—I took a photo by permission of this quilt as it hung on exhibition—but it was a failure because of the shadows. Arranged with a local photographer to take the picture after the Fair was over and have it properly lighted. The border of the quilt was rose calico, the spotted animals yellow & purple—the peacock black and white striped, the serpent black & yellow—having no feet in nature is here pictured the only thing with feet. Where Cain struck Abel the blood was red calico – The effect of these people & animals all punctured over with the most beautiful quilting …

"This colored woman was evidently 'color blind' or used only material at hand. I tried to buy the quilt but it was too valuable as an exhibit at fairs."[52]

---

[51] The Lee County Historical Society also owns a second, large-format photograph of the *Bible Quilt* that appears darker in exposure and has a different decorative frame. The creases and shadows on the quilt in this photograph are unique. It may be the "unsuccessful" image taken by Diver, though there seems to be no evidence confirming the name of the photographer.

[52] Lorene Diver, "A Sermon in Patchwork" photograph, no date though likely 1895 or 1896. Harriet Powers object file, National Museum of American History. According to the Textile Department, the photograph was a gift from a university, which knew the Smithsonian owned the *Bible Quilt*. Unfortunately, there doesn't appear to be any formal records noting which university, its date of acquisition or whether the photograph was part of a larger collection of images by Diver the university may have owned. The handwritten text on the back of the photograph is signed Lorene Curtis Diver. The handwriting and text on the Lee County Historical Society *Bible Quilt* photographs is practically identical to the Smithsonian copy.

Lorene Diver wrote a short, numbered description for each of the quilt's eleven blocks. It is unclear whether the descriptions are Diver's own or from place cards posted next to the quilt while it was on display in 1895. A few examples of what she wrote included:

"No.1   Adam & Eve in the garden of Eden—the serpent with feet black & yellow Original Sin—a dress form

No. 2   Adam & Eve & Cain in the Garden dove & animals

No. 3   Satan amid the Seven Stars

No. 4   Cain killing Abel. Cain was a shepherd—a stream of blood that flows over the Earth

No. 5   Cain when he went to the land of Nod to get him a wife—the spotted animal is a lion

No. 6   Jacobs' dream ladder angel descending"

Back side of A Sermon in Patchwork photo, ca. 1895-1896
Courtesy of the Lee County Historical Society, Keokuk, IA

The text is very similar to the Smithsonian copy text.

Oh, to see the *Bible Quilt* in person and in glorious color when it was first stitched! We know that two women, Jennie Smith and, now, Lorene Diver, wanted to own the quilt after being in its presence.

But, what did Diver mean when she wrote the *Bible Quilt* was "too valuable"? Was the quilt too valuable in a monetary sense or in a cultural sense? The Divers were financially well situated, as we will see. Therefore, I suspect, Jennie Smith had no intentions of selling the quilt, regardless of the offer price.

I also suspect, though I have no evidence, that Smith and Diver did not meet in person while Diver was in Atlanta. After all, what is the likelihood that Smith attended the Expo the same days Diver, from Keokuk, Iowa was there? Smith was most likely teaching her art classes at the Lucy Cobb Institute for much of the fair's run.

I suspect once Diver returned to Keokuk after visiting the Exposition she wrote to Jennie Smith in Athens to inquire about purchasing the *Bible Quilt* as Smith wrote the following to Diver:[53]

> Received of Harriet Powers a Biblical Quilt for which I gave her five dollars and enough calico to make another quilt.
>
> Jennie Smith
> September 1894[54]

---

[53] Copy of letter from Jennie Smith to Mrs. James B. Diver, Keokuk, Iowa in the Lorene C. Diver file, Lee County Historical Society. The letter appears to be a copy in Diver's hand. As it is a copy, I strongly suspect the correct date of the letter is 1895, after the Expo opened in September, and not 1894.

The Diver file is from the Raymond Everett Garrison collection. Garrison (1890 – 1980) was a noted local Keokuk historian, a reporter for the Daily Gate City (Keokuk, IA) newspaper, and editor of the Clinton, Iowa Advertiser. He worked for other publications, including spending seven years as sports editor of the Chicago Daily News and eight years at the Chicago Journal of Commerce. He retired and returned to Keokuk to live in 1948. He later wrote two books on Keokuk history. Lois Garrison (1896 – 1995), his second wife, was also a noted local historian and strong supporter of his work. See Garrison's obituary Daily Gate City, Aug. 20, 1980.

Diver had at least two copies of the professionally-taken *Bible Quilt* photograph made. She was likely a history enthusiast as she documented, in detail, the circumstances for taking the photograph in her own handwriting on the back of each image.

[54] I reviewed the Jennie Smith Papers at the Hargrett Rare Book & Manuscript Library at the University of Georgia, Athens before I knew about Lorene Curtis Diver. The Papers include five boxes of letters and other writings. I did not come across any reference to a quilt in the Papers. Nor do I recall any letter from Diver, although it is possible that one is in the Papers and I just did not realize its significance at the time. Additionally, if you are ever able to see the Papers in person, you'll see how difficult nineteenth-century cursive handwriting is to read at times. Jennie Smith's handwriting in her later years became a bit challenging to decipher.

If Jennie Smith sold the *Bible Quilt* to Lorene Diver, the fruits of Harriet Powers' hands would have moved to Iowa. Can you imagine? We might not even know of the *Bible Quilt* today if Diver had purchased the covering!

Lorene Diver, however, did not give up her quest to purchase the quilt. She eventually was able to learn Harriet Powers' mailing address and contacted her, probably on fine stationery with a two-cent postage stamp. Contrary to Clara R. Jemison's published assessment of Powers' social status, intelligence, and literary skills, *Mrs. Powers wrote back.*

Harriet A. Powers (1837—1910)

In February 2009, the decades-long forgotten Lorene Diver file at the Lee County Historical Society was opened. The contents of the file are groundbreaking and fundamentally change many of our perceptions of Harriet Powers and confirm she quilted more than just the two surviving quilts. The file treasures include a copy of the only known surviving letter from Harriet Powers. The handwritten copy appears to be in Lorene Diver's hand. The letter reads:[55]

---

[55] Copy of letter from Harriet A. Powers to Mrs. James B. Diver, Keokuk, Iowa in the Lorene C. Diver file, Lee County Historical Society. The copy is written in one long paragraph. I have broken the text into multiple paragraphs for easier readability. I also use the text "and" when an ampersand was used in the letter.

Athens, Ga
Jan 28th 1896

The life of Harriet Powers. Born in Madison Co. 8 miles from Athens on the Elberton road in the year Oct. 29, 1837. Her mistress was Nancy Lester. I commenced to learn at 11 years old and the white children learn me by sound on a poplar leaf. On Sundays after that I __ on books and done my own studying. I was married to Armsted Powers 1855. When I was free I moved to Dondy, Ga. In 1872 I made a quilt of 4 thousand and 50 diamonds.

In 1886 we moved to Athens and in 1887 I represented the star quilt in the colored fair association of Athens - Mr. Madison Davis, Pres, E. W. Bridy, clerk. The quilt of mine taken the premium.

In 1882 I became a member of Mt. Zion Baptist church. Then I visited Sunday school and read the Bible more than ever. Then I composed a quilt of the Lord's Supper from the New Testament. 2 thousand and 500 hundred diamonds.

In the year 1888, I composed and completed the quilt of Adam and Eve in the Garden of Eden—afterward sold it to Miss. Jennie Smith, and it was represented by her at the Exposition at Atlanta. I was there at the Ex – Dec. 26, 1896.[56]

I am the mother of 9 children—6 dead and 3 living. I am 58 years old.

After leaving Atlanta it was said I was dead—it was not so, for I was at the Exposition because I present the Governor of the colored department a watermelon Christmas Gift.[57] I am enjoying good health in Athens, Ga.

This I accomplish
Harriet A. Powers

---

[56] The letter appears to be a copy in Diver's handwriting. As it is a copy, I strongly suspect the correct date Harriet Powers visited the Exposition was 1895, not 1896 as the copy says. Additionally, the letter says the Garden of Eden quilt, which we know as the *Bible Quilt*, was completed in 1888. I strongly suspect the date is 1886, when it would have been displayed at the Cotton Fair. Note also the *Pictorial Quilt* does not seem to be listed here! Therefore, Harriet Powers stitched at least five quilts.

[57] Presumably the Governor of the Colored Department mentioned was I. Garland Penn, the head of the Negro Department. See The Life and Times of Irvine Garland Penn by Joanne and Grant Harrison (2000) for details on Penn. More research is needed to determine whether Penn kept a diary of events during the Exposition and possibly wrote about meeting Harriet Powers.

at the Exposition at Atlanta & I was
there at the Ex - Dec - 26, 1896
I am the mother of 9 children -
6 dead & 3 living. I am 58 years
old - After leaving Atlanta it was
said I was dead - it was not so
for I was at the Exposition becaus
I present the Governner of the
colored department a watermelon Crismas Gift - & I am en
joying good health in Athens Ga
                    This I accomplish
                        Harriet A Powers -

Copy - of No 2 -

   Received of Harriet Powers
a Biblical Quilt - for which I
gave her five dollars and
enough calico to make
an other quilt -
                    Jennie Smith
       September
              1894.

   Mrs James B. Diver -
            Keokuk
              Iowa -

Back side of letters in Lorene Curtis Diver's handwriting
Courtesy of the Lee County Historical Society, Keokuk, IA

In this one letter, Mrs. Harriet Angeline Powers sets straight her truths as a former slave and now free woman of accomplishment:

- She was literate
- She was healthy
- She was a wife and mother of nine children
- She stitched, to that time, at least four memorable quilts
- She was an exhibiting quilter
- She was an award-winning quilter
- She was a church-going, Bible-studying Christian
- She was acquainted with Black community organizers
- She traveled
- She was capable of representing her own artwork and communicating with potential collectors for herself

I just screamed and cried and screamed some more the first time I read Harriet Powers' letter to Lorene Diver. Who could have guessed the FedEx envelope Mrs. O'Connor sent me from Keokuk would include such an *unsearchable* treasure? So many thoughts swirled in my mind. I had assumed Harriet Powers was illiterate as other historians had. In this one letter, Sistah Quilter Harriet set us all straight! I had no doubt Powers wrote the original letter because the letter's contents were so deeply rooted in her community and experiences. The words rang true.

I wondered why Powers traveled to Atlanta to visit the Exposition the day after Christmas – why December 26? A trip to the Library of Congress solved this holiday mystery. This was Negro Day at the Exposition. It was advertised via "circulars, sermons and addresses." Workers and servants were given the day off to attend. Crowds of African Americans traveled from several states, including Illinois, to be present. The *Atlanta Constitution* estimated attendance at 30,000.[58] Black military troops paraded. Seven-year old Margarett Tate of Grand Rapids, Michigan recited the poem *We Are Coming*. Irvine Garland Penn, head of the Negro Building, addressed the gathering. There were also five-minute speeches by representatives of Atlanta University, Spelman Seminary, and other colleges. The Atlanta University Chorus provided the music. And, according to her own letter, Mrs. Harriet Powers attended.

---

[58] "This is Negro Day," Atlanta Constitution, Dec. 26, 1895, p. 5.

What did Powers think as she looked at the array of needlearts in the Negro Building? There was "an elaborate display of crochet and needlework" by women from Florida.[59] AME Bishop Henry Turner displayed his quilt featuring a coffee tree in full-bloom, a duplicate quilt Martha Ricks stitched for him based on one she made for Queen Victoria. Dr. Henry R. Butler wrote in the *Atlanta Constitution* of "a quilt, on which is worked the Lord's prayer. It is a good piece of hand-work, and should be seen by every visitor."[60] Irvine Garland Penn shared that "[i]n needlework the display is going to be extensive and the best. We should have one quilt there that the Afro-American owner wants $100 spot cash for."[61]

How did Powers feel seeing her *Bible Quilt* on display in the Negro Building? Did she smooth out a ripple on the quilt as it hung against a wall? Did she answer questions about the quilt for those who stopped by to view its beauty? Did she meet with anyone from Atlanta University who would later commission her to create another quilt?

I had no doubt about the veracity of the Powers letter to Lorene Diver. In fact, I started to cry and scream again as my eyes fell upon another sheet of paper from that FedEx package. The image in this photocopy was strangely familiar, yet distinctive. It was of Mrs. Powers.

Sometime in 1896 or 1897, Harriet Powers put on a dark, long-skirted dress and donned a white apron with appliquéd symbols. She pinned a favorite brooch to her laced collar. She ventured from her home to 115 Broad Street in downtown Athens and walked into the portrait studio of Charles F. McDannell to have her photograph taken.

McDannell started advertising in the *Southern Banner*, an Athens newspaper, for photographs and photo-engraving services in 1897.[62] Powers purchased *carte de visite* images of herself. These 2 ¼" x 3 ¾"

---

[59] Harrison, The Life and Times of Irvine Garland Penn, p. 78.

[60] H.R. Butler, no title, The Atlanta Constitution, Oct. 6, 1895, p. 17. Butler wrote an ongoing column about African American life.

[61] "The New Negro at Our Show," The Atlanta Constitution, July 28, 1895, p. 4. The purchasing power of $100 in 1895 is $2,645 in 2008, according to MeasuringWorth.com.

[62] Special thanks to Dr. W. Robert Nix, Professor Emeritus of Art, University of Georgia, Athens for sharing his research on Athens Georgia Artist/Photographers 1839– 1939 and on McDannell with me. McDannell's business directory listing can be found in the Southern Banner, the local Athens newspaper, September 10, 17, 24, 1897 issues. The photographers Harris & Bloomfield advertised services from a 115 Broad Street studio in March– August 1897, according to Dr. Nix.

prints were popular calling cards of the day. The *carte de visite* process required a camera with four lenses. The photographer could take four identical or four different pictures on one half of a plate. As a result, one could obtain eight identical or different photographs per entire plate.[63]

We don't know what prompted Powers to have her portrait taken. We do know that she ordered multiple copies. One was given to Dr. Charles C. Hall, who received her *Pictorial Quilt* in 1898 as a gift. This photograph remains framed and under glass at the Museum of Fine Arts, Boston.[64] One copy was sent to Lorene Diver in Keokuk and is now owned by the Lee County Historical Society.[65] From our perspective in the twenty-first century, Harriet Powers' use of the *carte de visite* is much like our use of an artist's resume or Facebook profile; we want to make sure actual and potential buyers of our artwork know who we are.

Harriet Powers, circa 1896—1897
Courtesy of the Lee County Historical Society, Keokuk, IA

---

[63] O. Henry Mace, "The Carte de Visite Process," in <u>Collector's Guide to Early Photographs</u> (Radnor, PA: Wallace-Homestead Book Company, 1989), pp. 115–117.

[64] I bet the Museum of Fine Arts, Boston Powers photograph also has a McDannell Studio stamp, though I don't recall ever seeing the studio's stamp or a photographer credit given for this image.

[65] It is unknown whether Powers included the *carte de visite* in the 1896 letter to Diver or sent the photograph in a subsequent letter. It's unclear if McDannell operated his 115 Broad Street studio in 1886. If he did not, this may suggest a continued correspondence between Diver and Powers.

Back side of Harriet Powers photograph, circa 1896—1897
Courtesy of the Lee County Historical Society, Keokuk, IA
The handwriting appears to be from Lorene Curtis Diver.

Did Lorene Diver, who was financially well-situated, ever commission a quilt from Harriet Powers? There are no indications that Lorene Diver continued to communicate with either Smith or Powers—or rather, none yet found!

Lorene and James Diver continued to pursue their love of new places. From 1906 to 1907, the couple literally traveled the world logging 42,000 miles and visiting twenty-six countries, including Macoa, China, Madras, India, Wrexham, Wales, and London, England.[66] She continued to take photographs and share the images during her club meetings.[67]

Community enrichment was a major focus for Diver. Today one can visit Rand Park in Keokuk, look at the base of the statue honoring Chief Keokuk (1767—1848) and read Diver's name among the eight Daughters of the American Revolution committee members responsible for erecting the statue in 1913.

Also in 1913, Diver published a booklet titled *To Sound Waves*, describing the thunderous reverberations heard from her Port Sunshine home of the Dam and Power House (Lock and Dam #19) being

---

[66] Reeves, <u>The Blue Book of Iowa Women</u>, p. 146.

[67] Garrison, <u>Goodbye My Keokuk Lady</u>, p. 88.

constructed nearby on the Mississippi River. Her husband, James, was an engineer on the dam project.

Talking with friends while leaving a Daughters of the American Revolution meeting at a member's house, Lorene Diver, now seventy-one years old, accidentally tripped down stone steps and hit her head with stunning force. She didn't tell her husband what had happened. He found out from others the following day. Sadly, the fall caused Diver, the amateur photographer who once wanted to purchase the *Bible Quilt* after seeing it, to go blind within the year. By all accounts, James Diver lovingly cared for his wife and became her eyes until she passed away five years later in 1922.[68]

In November 1929, eleven months before he died, James Diver signed his last will and testament in the presence of two witnesses.[69] In his will, he outlined the creation of the Lorene Curtis Diver Memorial Fund to benefit the Trinity Methodist Episcopal Church of Keokuk. James could not bear the thought of anyone else living in Port Sunshine, the home he shared with Lorene, or disposing of their property. He wrote that the home contained "complete household furnishing, and modern in equipment, Books, many of them rare and valuable editions, Pictures, Photographs, Coins, Old Currency, Articles and Curios from the world over, and many others too numerous to mention."

James Diver directed the Memorial Fund to support the maintenance of Port Sunshine and its Trustee, who would live there, from the income of his other properties. The first Trustee was Amelia Buttschau Smith, who moved into Port Sunshine and lived there until she passed away in the mid-1950s. The subsequent Trustees eventually sold various Diver properties. On September 19, 1959, the contents of Port Sunshine were sold at auction. Eleven-year old Louisa Kiedaisch purchased a full-size treadle sewing machine for just 25 cents. The entire auction brought in $1,000 for the fund.[70] I have not (yet) been able to locate an inventory of

---

[68] Garrison, Goodbye My Keokuk Lady, pp. 91 – 92. For Lorene Diver's obituary, see "Death Today of Mrs. J. B. Diver," Daily Gate City (Keokuk, IA), June 7, 1922, p. 9.

[69] Will of James Brice Diver, Keokuk, IA, Nov. 27, 1929. South Lee County Court and County Offices, Keokuk, IA.

[70] See Raymond E. Garrison, Tales of Early Keokuk Homes, pages 118 – 119 for details.

There appears to be no explanation as to why Garrison had copies of documents and photos related to Lorene C. Diver and the *Bible Quilt.* Garrison did write an essay about Diver in his book, Goodbye My Keokuk Lady, though he did not write about the *Bible Quilt.*

the auction to learn whether any of Lorene Diver's correspondence, diaries, photographs, or quilts were sold.

The Lorene Curtis Diver Memorial Fund still earns interest today.

African Americans in Jennie Smith's Life

From Lorene Diver, we know Jennie Smith turned down one offer to buy the *Bible Quilt*. What many quilt historians don't know, though, is that the *Bible Quilt* was not the only piece of artwork by an African American that Jennie Smith admired, retained, and touched.

Sometime in 1886, a young girl picked up a pencil and sketched bold drawings of black birds and men with top hats in the margins of a literary magazine. One may gaze on the young girl's drawings and be reminded of the style of Alabama folk artist Bill Traylor (1854—1949).

Drawings by Rhoda Ann, Athens, GA, about 1886
Courtesy of Hargrett Rare Book and Manuscript Library,
University of Georgia Libraries

There are at least two possible scenarios that explain why Garrison had the documents and photos. The first is that Lorene Diver made the handwritten copies for Raymond Garrison at some point before she died in 1922. I suspect that throughout Garrison's life, he collected interesting stories about his boyhood town and neighbors, including Diver. The second theory is that Garrison purchased the items in the 1959 auction. In this case, though, I do not understand why Garrison would have a copy of the Harriet Powers and Jennie Smith letters in Lorene Diver's handwriting and not the originals.

Smith forgot she had the drawings for more than forty years. Then, suddenly, she stumbled upon them one day. When she did, she didn't crumble and discard the pictures. Instead, she wrote a note documenting the young Black girl's creation, which she kept until her death.

Smith wrote on the backside of the paper: "Drawings made by negro girl, Rhoda Ann, maid of Miss Jennie Smith's, about 1886. They look modern now and like the African primitive art (which it was). Found when looking over clippings in 1928."[71]

Who was Rhoda Ann? The 1880 U.S. Census lists two different African American girls named Rhoda from Clarke County, Buck Branch, the community near where Jennie Smith lived. One was Rhoda Colbert, age 13, and the other Rhoda A. Sherman, age 11. There is no other information about Rhoda Ann to give us a clue as to which girl, if either, may have been her maid.

Did Rhoda Ann continue to draw and create? Did Smith have an emotional connection with Rhoda Ann or an emotional connection with her art that caused her to keep the drawings for sixty years?

Rhoda Ann and Harriet Powers, though, were not the only African Americans with whom Jennie Smith had a relationship.

Over the decades, Smith made numerous trips to Paris to visit friends and study art. She traveled across the Atlantic Ocean to France in 1904. That year, Josephine Micking wrote at least two letters to her friend Jennie Smith.[72] Micking's letters are chatty and reference common acquaintances. The letters are written in a large cursive style using a pencil. The content is adult, but the writing style seems like that of one who was not practiced in writing and who sometimes misspelled words, including her own name.

The Jennie Smith Papers appear to contain no information clarifying who Josephine Micking might be. The 1900 and 1910 U.S. Census list an African American woman named Josephine Mickens in Athens. Piecing

---

[71] Jennie Smith Papers, MSS 13, Box 3:3. Courtesy of the Hargrett Rare Book & Manuscript Library, University of Georgia Libraries. I am confident Smith wrote the description as the handwriting matches the hundreds of pages of notes by Smith in the Papers. The handwriting also matches Jennie Smith's written description of the *Bible Quilt* at the Smithsonian. No other drawings by African Americans appear to be included in the Papers.

[72] Josephine Micking to Jennie Smith, June 1 (no year) and July 1, 1904, MSS 13, Box 1:2, Jennie Smith Papers. Hargrett Rare Book & Manuscript Library, University of Georgia. From the content of the letters, Smith wrote at least one letter to Micking (or Mickens) on June 21, 1904.

together other federal and state data, Josephine Mickens was a cook married to Dock Mickens, a cotton baler. She died in 1939 at the age of fifty-six.

What is remarkable about one of Micking's letters is that she shared an endearing aspiration with Jennie Smith. She wrote:

"...i wish i was over in Paris just a half and hour if not longer

ever thing getting a long all rite

I will close from

your survan Josephine"[73]

Oh, the dreams of this domestic black woman in 1904! What news of Paris did she receive in Athens, Georgia? The celebrated African American performer, Josephine Baker, had not even been born yet. Had Mrs. Micking ever heard French spoken? Did she wish to see the Eiffel Tower, which opened to great fanfare and worldwide publicity in 1889?

Jennie Smith Continues to Promote the Art of Others

Jennie Smith was a nineteenth-century marketer. Over the years she actively sought recognition for her Lucy Cobb Institute students beyond Athens' city limits. She exhibited her students artwork at the 1895 Cotton States and International Exposition in Atlanta. In 1903, she wrote to Edward William Bok (1863—1930), editor of the *Ladies Home Journal,* to request that the magazine offer a prize for poster artwork created by her students. William V. Alexander, managing editor for the magazine, responded to say it would be more interested in judging artwork with potential for the magazine's cover. Eventually, Bok awarded a $25 prize to one of Smith's students.[74] In 1907, the Packer Manufacturing Company, makers of Packer's Tar Soap, gave three monetary prizes to

---

[73] Josephine Micking to Jennie Smith, July 1, 1904, MSS 13, Box 1:2, Jennie Smith Papers, Hargrett Rare Book & Manuscript Library, University of Georgia Libraries. One wonders whether Micking's (or Mickens) extended family knows these letters are at the University of Georgia.

[74] Wm. V. Alexander to Jennie Smith, MSS 13, Box 1:2, Jennie Smith Papers,. Hargrett Rare Book & Manuscript Library, University of Georgia Libraries.

Smith's art students as well as purchased selected artwork for its New York corporate office.[75]

There seems to be no evidence, yet rediscovered, that Smith exhibited the *Bible Quilt* after the 1895 Cotton States and International Exposition.

In January 1910, Harriet Powers passed away at the age of seventy-two. She was buried at the local African American burial grounds, the Gospel Pilgrim Cemetery, and laid to rest besides her husband Armsted, who died just months before.

Later in the year, Jennie Smith petitioned the Lucy Cobb Institute to allow her to live on the school's grounds for the remainder of her life in a brick cottage, which had been the cook's house. Permission was granted, and the house was remodeled to accommodate living spaces and an art studio.[76]

The *Bible Quilt* seemed to stay out of the news until 1914.

Lucine Finch (1875—1947)

In 1914, *Outlook*, a weekly journal edited by Rev. Dr. Lyman Abbott (1835—1922) published "A Sermon in Patchwork," an article about the *Bible Quilt* written by Lucine Finch.

Finch was born about 1875 to Julia Neely Finch (1853—1926) and Edwin Wilson Finch (1850—1899?). She grew up primarily in New Orleans and Birmingham, Alabama. One family servant, an African American woman, cared for the Finch family for three generations.[77] Finch would earn a living, in part, from the stories she heard from this family servant.

Finch attended the University of Chicago from about 1905 to 1910 and studied dramatic arts. One newspaper reported that "[t]hose who have laughed over her dramatic monologues will not forget her powers of

---

[75] Packer's Manufacturing Co., Edward A. Olds, Proprietor, to Jennie Smith, MSS 13, Box 1:3, Jennie Smith Papers. Hargrett Rare Book & Manuscript Library, University of Georgia Libraries.

[76] Spalding, Higher Education for Women in the South, p. 44. Today Smith's cottage still stands. It has been remodeled as office space. Lovely photographs of the cottage from when Smith lived there are located in the Jennie Smith Papers.

[77] "Miss Finch Dies, Noted Dramatist of Negro Stories," Hartford Courant, Mar. 19, 1947, p. 4.

negro mimicry and spontaneous humor. She travels all over the country and has been successful in vaudeville houses of the east."[78]

During her life Finch had several short stories published including "Aunt 'Liza One of the Slaves Who Stayed" (*American Magazine*, Feb. 1909), "The Boy at the Window" (*Harper's Monthly Magazine,* Oct. 1914), "Slaves Who Stayed: Mammy" (*American Magazine*, Sept. 1907), "Slaves Who Stayed: Phil's Tom" (*American Magazine*, Dec. 1907), "The Spirit in the Old House" (*Ladies Home Journal,* May 1912), and "Uncle Carter of the Peg-Leg: A Sketch from Life" (*Century Illustrated Monthly Magazine*, May 1908). She also wrote and illustrated the poetry book *Two in Arcadia* published in 1907 by Brentanos. A five-page handwritten short story by Finch titled "The Darkey and the Deed: A (nig) Heroic Tale" is located at the Birmingham Public Library.

Over the years, Lucine Finch performed a signature creation titled "Her Mammy's Stories," based on religious tales and songs from her family servant. Chicago *Record-Herald* literary and drama critic James O'Donnell Bennett wrote passionately of one performance:[79]

"… she held the people to rapt attention for an hour and a half with her retelling of negro folk tales and birdlike caroling of real negro melodies.

"Sitting in an old-fashioned armchair and bending forward in an intimate way, she reeled off story after story in a rich, unctuous tone and with an eloquence of gesticulation that was the best kind of action, because it was so spontaneous, so appropriate, and so evidently from nature. No jangling piano accompanied the songs….The gyrations and waddlings as of an epileptic cake walker were not introduced, nor was there any rude bawling or horrible mouthing, such as the average vaudeville performer employs when he attempts a negro impersonation."

---

[78] "Does Higher Education Dwarf an Artistic Temperament?" Chicago Daily Tribune, Feb. 27, 1910, p. G2. The article does not mention if she graduated from the school. Photo included.

[79] In "Lucine Finch in Her Mammy's Stories Unpublished Religious Songs of the Old South," undated performance program, though likely after 1910. Photograph of Finch on cover. Interestingly, I purchased an autographed program on eBay in 2008. There are also two copies of the program at the Lake Erie College Archives in Painesville, OH. Finch was a performer and drama coach there in 1912 and 1913, according to an April 28, 2009 email to the author from Chris Bennett, Director of Lincoln Library at Lake Erie College.

I first read Lucine Finch's 1914 article about Harriet Powers' *Bible Quilt* nearly ten years ago when I was in my thirties, making story quilts in earnest, and hoping one of my quilts would be appreciated a hundred years in the future like Powers' own two known surviving quilts. I read "A Sermon in Patchwork" and was furious!

As a Christian, an African American woman, a quilter, and admirer of Powers, "A Sermon in Patchwork" offended me for several reasons. First, Finch seemed to disrespect Harriet Powers. Next, she seemed to both revere and dismiss the *Bible Quilt* in the same sentences. Finally, she seemed to disrespect African Americans in general.

Lucine Finch – undated photograph
Source: Library of Congress Prints & Photographs, Washington, D.C

"A Sermon in Patchwork" described the *Bible Quilt* based on a full-size photograph of the piece.[80] Finch didn't seem to recognize Harriet Powers' personhood or equality in her article. She never once provided the reader with Powers' name or physical description. Instead, she called her, among other adjectives, "an aged Negro woman." In the article's first paragraph, she wrote of Powers:

> "Her idea was, as she voices it, "to preach a sermon in patchwork." In other words, to express through this humble and homely medium the qualities of mind and soul that are the inborn possession of the Negro – the leveling of all events to his personal conception of them, and the free, colorful imagination of a primitive mind... In order fully to comprehend the wonderful imagination wrought in mystic symbols into this old quilt one must really know something about the Negro himself, more especially about the "old timey" Negro, who is so fast and so tragically disappearing."[81]

Lucine Finch didn't write how she came to know about the *Bible Quilt* or when she presumably interviewed Powers, who passed away four years before the article was published. Of Powers, Finch wrote that "I shall use her own words, in as far as I can quote them."

Finch then provided quotes, presumably from Powers, in a stereotypical dialect. For example, Finch wrote that the quiltmaker explained why the Devil held a star in one of the quilt blocks by saying "elusively, 'dar ain't no tellin' dat, chile; no tellin' dat.'" In another instance Finch presumably asked Powers to explain her fabric choice in the Jacob's ladder block. Powers, she wrote, said "whimsically, 'I couldn't turn myself loose in color, honey! De animals' calico 'blige ter run over in a de ladder. Dar wa'n't no yuther way.'"

The quotes Finch published don't read or sound like the dignified, confident, or accomplished Harriet A. Powers who wrote to Lorene Curtis Diver of Keokuk, Iowa. Had Finch even met Powers?

In 1914, Finch was thirty-nine years old. She had performed "Her Mammy's Stories" a number of times. The quotes attributed to Powers in

---

[80] Lucine Finch, "A Sermon in Patchwork," Outlook, Oct. 28, 1914, pp. 493 – 495. One can find the article on books.google.com. http://books.google.com/books?id=4YPHt27j4zwC

[81] Finch, "A Sermon in Patchwork," p. 493.

the Sermon article seemed to use the same "negro impersonation" technique as a character in her monologues.

In the article, Finch didn't seem to respect African Americans. She wrote that the "Negro's mind is the child's mind; is the savage, original, spontaneous outputting of the divine."

A couple times she referred to the *Bible Quilt* as "the old quilt." She said "the old quilt pictured herewith...is the reverent, worshipful embodiment of an old colored woman's soul." She later wrote that "[t]here is a certain wistfulness about the old quilt that touches something fine in us."

But did Lucine Finch ever really touch the *Bible Quilt*? Where did she get the photograph of the quilt for the 1914 article? There is no photographic credit listed in the article or elsewhere in the magazine.

I have a theory, admittedly with no concrete evidence to support it. I suspect Finch obtained a copy of one of Lorene Diver's professional photographs of the *Bible Quilt* with Diver's handwritten notes on the back of the photograph. As a result, Finch used Diver's notes as a basis to describe the *Bible Quilt* and "quote" Harriet Powers.[82]

Why would I think this? The title of the 1914 article is "A Sermon in Patchwork," which is coincidentally the same title Lorene Diver wrote on her 1895-96 photographs of the *Bible Quilt*. Additionally, how Finch described the eleven quilt blocks is nearly identical to what Diver wrote on the back of her photo. You can see below that Finch's description of the first three blocks is just like Diver's, with minor grammatical variations:

"1. Adam and Eve in the Garden of Eden. The serpent with feet, black and yellow. Original Sin, a dress form.

2. Adam and Eve and Cain in the Garden. Dove and animals.

3. Satan amid the Seven Stars."

---

[82] The "Sermon in Patchwork" photograph with Lorene Diver's notes now owned by the Smithsonian was a gift. The paperwork for the photograph is not available and maybe misfiled. The Textile Department recalls that the photograph may have been a gift from a university library in Alabama (source: Jan. 5, 2009 email to the author). It will be exciting to learn, if possible, whether the gift source had any connections to Lucine Finch or Lorene Diver.

I believe that Lorene Diver wrote her notes about seeing the *Bible Quilt* in the Negro Building on the back of the photographs of the quilt in 1895-96. In her enthusiasm to purchase the *Bible Quilt*, I doubt Diver would have hired a professional photographer to capture the quilt's image, corresponded with both Jennie Smith and Harriet Powers directly after seeing the *Bible Quilt* in person, then wait eighteen years to stumble upon Finch's 1914 article about the quilt and copy Finch's quilt descriptions on the back of her own 1895-96 photographs.

Perhaps we'll never know for sure whether Lucine Finch actually touched the *Bible Quilt* or met Powers in person. Perhaps we'll never know who gave her the *Bible Quilt* photograph for the article.

In 1929 Lucine Finch was still performing her "Mammy Stories," according to the *New York Times*.[83] During the administration of President Herbert Hoover (1929—1933), Finch was requested to give a performance at the White House.[84] In 1931, she hosted a weekly fifteen-minute radio program on WJZ-760 in New York called "Stories of the Old South."[85]

From about 1928 to the early 1940s, Finch lived in Greenwich, Connecticut. She taught at the private Edgewood School and directed its drama students in an annual Nativity play. Finch also operated an antiques/gift store called the Little Shop at 12 West Putnam Avenue with her long-time friend, housemate, and partner Clare Hamilton (1878—1973), an English woman born in India.[86] Over the years, Hamilton also taught music, including piano, in private schools.[87] The Little Shop, according to the local Greenwich newspaper, was "a center for the expression of [Lucine Finch's] artistic talent."[88]

---

[83] "Coulter D. Huylers Are Hosts," New York Times, June 22, 1929, p. 24.

[84] "Miss Finch Dies, Noted Dramatist of Negro Stories," Hartford Courant, Mar. 19, 1947. White House social activities during the Hoover years were handled by the First Lady's personal secretary. As a result, there are no "official" records of White House performances, according to Spencer Howard, Herbert Hoover Presidential Library, in an Apr. 27, 2009 email to the author.

[85] "Today on the Radio," New York Times, May 21, 1931, p. 36. Also listed on May 28. It is unclear whether any tape recordings of Finch's radio program still exist.

[86] Greenwich, Connecticut City Directories 1928, 1937, 1939, and 1941. Hamilton operated the shop at least through 1953, according to City Directories

[87] "Clare Hamilton," Greenwich Time, May 30, 1973. Obituary for Miss Hamilton.

[88] "Lucine Finch Dies in West Hartford," Greenwich Time, Mar. 20, 1947, p. 2:1.

Lucine Finch passed away in 1947 in a West Hartford, Connecticut convalescent home at the age of seventy-two. She was buried with her family at the Oak Hill Cemetery in Birmingham, Alabama.

Jennie Smith Celebrates Golden Years

At the 1930 Lucy Cobb Institute graduation ceremony, Jennie Smith was honored for fifty years of service to the school and its students. She was sixty-eight years old.

During the ceremony, Willis Henry Bocock (1865—1947), professor of Classics at the University of Georgia, surprised Jennie Smith by formally presenting her with a golden-colored basket filled with a bundle of yellow flowers to mark her Golden Jubilee. Many friends and former students from across the country contributed to a gift tucked into a decorative, locked box inside the flowers: a gift of $700 in gold coins.[89]

Jennie Smith posing with her Golden Jubilee Basket, 1930
Courtesy of Hargrett Rare Book & Manuscript Library,
University of Georgia Libraries.

---

[89] Spalding, <u>Higher Education for Women in the South: A History of Lucy Cobb Institute 1858 – 1994</u>, (Athens: Georgia Southern Press, 1994), p. 44. The purchasing power of $700 in 1930 is $9,024 in 2008 dollars according to MeasuringWorth.com.

The Class of 1930 was the last to graduate from the Lucy Cobb Institute as the school then closed in the face of declining admissions and increased competition for young girls from co-educational colleges. Smith, who had first come to its campus as a student, taught art there for fifty years, and had lived in a cottage behind the Institute's main building since 1910, continued to reside in her small house and studio.

On January 4, 1946, at the age of eighty-three, Jennie Smith signed her last will and testament in the presence of three witnesses.[90] Sadly, she passed away in her home only two months later. Her funeral services were held at Emmanuel Episcopal Church in Athens. Afterward, she was buried near her parents and brother, Wales Wynton, in the Oconee Hill Cemetery.[91]

She entrusted Harold M. Heckman, her executor, to settle her estate.

Harold M. Heckman (1899—1987)

Harold Milton Heckman was born on February 15, 1899 in Bradford, Massachusetts. He attended the University of Arizona as an undergraduate and Columbia University for his master's degree. He was a CPA and later member of the Georgia Bar. His University of Georgia, Athens teaching career spanned forty-five years, beginning in 1921.[92]

Heckman had two children. He and his wife, Julia Tyler, had a daughter, Jeanne, about 1923. Sadly, Julia passed away ten days after Jeanne was born.[93] He later married a "local girl" named Claudia Flanigen and had a son, Harold Heckman, Jr.

Who knows when Heckman first met Jennie Smith. Perhaps it was at the Emmanuel Episcopal Church, where Heckman was an active member of long-standing. Or maybe it was through his wife Claudia, who graduated with the Class of 1919 at the Lucy Cobb Institute.[94]

---

[90] Will of Miss Jennie Smith, Will Book H, 1940 – 1955, Athens, Clarke County, GA.

[91] Moselle S. Weston. "Miss Jennie Smith," Athens Banner (GA), Mar. 17, 1946. See also "Funeral Notice – Smith," Banner-Herald (Athens, GA), Mar. 14, 1946, p. 3.

[92] "An Endowed Chair in Public Accounting to Honor Harold M. Heckman," brochure, University of Georgia, J. M. Tull School of Accounting, undated, likely 1983.

[93] "Jeanne Greenleaf Nurse, Artist, Musician," Portland Press Herald (ME), June 14, 1997, p. 9B.

[94] Spalding, Higher Education for Women in the South, p. 118.

Professor Harold M. Heckman
Courtesy of the University of Georgia, J.M. Tull School of Accounting

In my research I spoke with several older Athens residents who knew Harold Heckman. Each spoke highly of his integrity, sense of responsibility and helpfulness. Each said in a unique way that Heckman was a "good man." One Athens resident said Heckman "was a wonderful man, though he had a gruff manner. If you had a friend in Hal Heckman, you had a friend."[95]

Heckman used his accounting skills to assist older members in the Athens community with their personal finances and/or annual income taxes, according to extended family members.[96]

In 1946, Heckman became Jennie Smith's executor when he was forty-seven years old.

According to the literature about the *Bible Quilt*, Harriet Powers offered to sell the quilt to Jennie Smith for $10. Unfortunately, Smith could not afford the asking price and offered $5 instead. Powers accepted the money in 1891. Smith's financial situation improved in later years.

When Smith's will was read, seventeen individuals learned she bequeathed each a monetary gift ranging from $100 to $3,500. In total,

---

95 Name withheld, telephone interview with Kyra E. Hicks, Sept. 14, 2008.

96 Names withheld, two separate telephone interviews with Kyra E. Hicks, Oct. 1, 2008.

she gave \$12,150.[97] One gift of \$400 was designated for a Lucy Williams, "[i]f she is in my service at the time of my death." The 1930 U.S. Census for Clarke County, Georgia lists two women named Lucy Williams. Each is an African American woman.

The United Daughters of the Confederacy (in memorial for Miss Millie Rutherford, former principal of the Lucy Cobb Institute), the Salvation Army, and the "Poor of Athens" also received monetary gifts.

Heckman, his wife Claudia, and fourteen-year-old son Hal Jr. each received a monetary gift from Smith. His daughter, Jeanne, who was twenty-three years old, was not listed in the will. She was probably not living in Athens at that time. She attended Maryville College in Tennessee at the age of sixteen and then went to Columbia University for her nursing degree.[98]

After the Lucy Cobb Institute closed in 1930-31, the University of Georgia, Athens leased the school's property to house women students.[99] The University allowed Smith to continue living on campus in the brick carriage house behind the main building. Perhaps in gratitude, Smith bequeathed specific gifts to the University:

> "I leave my piano to the New Library of the University of Georgia. China Closet, Library Carved Table, Antique Writing Desk, Round Duncan Phyfe Table and Sofa."[100]

The literature about the *Bible Quilt* usually says that the quilt was not mentioned specifically in Jennie Smith's will. This is true.

Smith asked her dear friend Anne Wallis Brumby (1876—1964) to "superintend the distribution of my personal property."[101] Brumby

---

[97] Will of Miss Jennie Smith, item vi. The purchasing power of \$12,150 in 1946 is \$133,875 in 2008 dollars according to MeasuringWorth.com.

[98] "Jeanne Greenleaf Nurse, Artist, Musician," Portland Press Herald (ME), June 14, 1997, p. 9B.

[99] Spalding, Higher Education for Women in the South: A History of Lucy Cobb Institute 1858 – 1994, (Athens: Georgia Southern Press, 1994), pp. 49, 273 – 275.

[100] Will of Miss Jennie Smith, item viii. The piano is today on display in the Memorial Room of the Carl Vinson Institute of Government (former Lucy Cobb Institute building) in Athens. Special thanks to Dan Evans, Facilities Manager, for confirming this via April 29, 2009 email. The piano is gorgeous, if you have an opportunity to visit the restored Lucy Cobb Institute building.

[101] Will of Miss Jennie Smith, item vii. Smith spelled Anne Brumby's first name as "Ann" in the will. It is unclear whether a personal diary from Anne Brumby exists or if she would have even written about dispersing Smith's personal items. Brumby was the sister of Mary Harris Brumby

graduated from the Lucy Cobb Institute in 1892. She was the Associate Principal at the Institute from 1908 to 1917. She later served as Dean of Women from 1924 to 1929 at the University of Georgia. Smith lived in her home thirty-six years. As anyone who has ever had the sad task of clearing a loved one's possessions knows, distributing personal effects is not easy and can be emotional. There are no records, yet found, on how Anne Brumby handled this task.

Jennie Smith's last request in her will stated:

> "All the residue of my property of whatever character, real or personal, whether now owned or hereafter acquired… I will to the University of Georgia, to be used for the New Library, preferably the interest to be used for new books."[102]

"Oh, my God!" I screamed the first time I read this passage of Smith's will. My hands shook. For a moment, I couldn't believe it. Did I just read that the remains of Jennie Smith's estate were to go to the University of Georgia? Did that include the *Bible Quilt?*

Did Harold Heckman or his wife Claudia receive the *Bible Quilt* as a "distribution" from Anne Brumby? Or, should the *Bible Quilt*, as "residue," have become the property of the University of Georgia?

Would a sixty-year-old quilt, no matter how unusual, even be an object one would consider valuable enough to distribute or perhaps sell to benefit the University of Georgia?

Did a representative of the University ever say the institution did not want the *Bible Quilt?*[103] Would a university that would not admit its first African American students (Charlayne Hunter-Gault and Hamilton Holmes) until 1961 care about a story quilt by a local Black resident?

Heckman was ten years old and living in Massachusetts when Harriet Powers passed away. Smith's own documentation about the *Bible Quilt* only mentioned the quiltmaker's first name. In 1946, would Heckman

---

and Admiral Frank Hardeman Brumby. See "Admiral Brumby Dies in Norfolk, 75," New York Times, July 17, 1950. See photo of Jennie and Anne in Remembering Athens by Susan Tate.

[102] Will of Miss Jennie Smith, item ix.

[103] The Georgia Museum of Art, which is housed on the campus of the University of Georgia, Athens opened to the public in 1948, two years after Jennie Smith passed away.

have even thought to seek out the children or grandchildren of Harriet Powers to give or sell the quilt back to her family?

I have absolutely no doubts about Harold Heckman's integrity and trust he knew Jennie Smith so well as to understand her intentions for her estate. Heckman's actions regarding the *Bible Quilt* preserved a future national treasure.

So, then, how did Harriet Powers' *Bible Quilt* get to the Smithsonian?

I have tried unsuccessfully to secure first-person accounts of the *Bible Quilt* while it was with the Heckman family. Heckman passed away in 1987. His second wife, Claudia, died in 1976. His son, Hal Jr., to whom Smith bequeathed a monetary gift in her will, grew up and became a First Lieutenant in the Air Force. Once he left the service, he returned to Athens and considered going back to school. He took a trip to New York to visit graduate programs there. Returning home to Athens, he died tragically in a 1959 commercial plane crash outside of Baltimore.[104]

Jeanne Heckman Greenleaf, Heckman's oldest daughter who may have even known Jennie Smith, survived her parents and brother. She became a nurse, a musician, and author of the romance novel *Above All, Love* (1984). I wondered if she could tell me why Smith trusted Heckman to be her trustee. Maybe she could tell me how the *Bible Quilt* was cared for by her parents – was it tucked away in a trunk or displayed on the bed in the guest bedroom. Maybe she would even tell me whether she ever slept under the *Bible Quilt*. Unfortunately, I wasn't able to meet her in time. She passed away in Asheboro, North Carolina in 1997.[105]

In the summer of 1968, twenty-two years after Jennie Smith passed away, William Porter Kellam (1905—1993), Director of Libraries for the University of Georgia, Athens, was in Washington, D.C. for some reason. He took time out of his schedule to visit the Smithsonian's National Museum of History and Technology. He spent a few moments speaking with one of the secretaries at the museum's Textile Department about "a biblical quilt which a friend of mine wishes to place in a museum… He also has a tree of life coverlet."[106]

---

[104] Harold Heckman, Jr., twenty-six other passengers and four crew members on Capital Airlines Flight 75 passed away on May 12, 1959 when the plane went down in extreme turbulence.

[105] Jeanne Greenleaf Nurse, Artist, Musician," Portland Press Herald (ME), June 14, 1997, p. 9B.

[106] W.P. Kellam to Doris Bowman, July 8, 1968. Item no. 283472.004, Textile Department, Smithsonian National Museum of American History. Kellam also enclosed "an article" about the

Doris M. Bowman, then Lace and Needlework Specialist at the museum, was out of the office and missed Kellam's visit. She later wrote to him that the museum would be interested in examining both quilts and enclosed a mailing label to cover shipping costs.[107]

In October, after spending the summer in Newburyport, Massachusetts visiting family, Heckman mailed the *Bible Quilt* and a Tree of Life patterned quilt to Bowman.[108] In a letter to her, Heckman explained his motivation for sending the quilts:

> "I believe both these quilts should be retained for general benefit. I know of no place I would prefer to the Smithsonian. Mrs. Heckman and I would be most happy should the Institute accept these items."[109]

Heckman, who was now sixty-nine years old, and his wife had owned the *Bible Quilt* for more than two decades. He was recently retired from a distinguished teaching career at the University of Georgia. How did he feel touching the *Bible Quilt* one last time before he mailed it?

When the *Bible Quilt* arrived via the United States Postal Service, Bowman later recalled how amazed she and the Textile Department staff were when they first unfolded the quilt:

> "It just came in the mail and we opened it and we were just floored....It was so different from anything we had ever seen."[110]

Bible Quilt with this letter. From later correspondences, the "article" seemed to be Jennie Smith's essay about the quilt and Harriet Powers' descriptions of the quilt blocks. See also Bowman's letter to Mr. & Mrs. H. M. Heckman, Oct. 22, 1968.

[107] Doris M. Bowman to W. P. Kellam, July 11, 1968, Item no. 283472.002, Textile Department, Smithsonian National Museum of American History.

[108] The Tree of Life quilt, according to Heckman, "had many pins in it where the woman who owned it planned to sew. Being over 90 years of age she never did get to this work." He did not name the quiltmaker. Harold Heckman to Doris M. Bowman, Oct. 14, 1968, Item no. 283472.003, Textile Department, Smithsonian National Museum of American History. The 110" x 103.5" appliquéd quilt was stitched circa 1830.

[109] Harold Heckman to Doris M. Bowman, Oct. 14, 1968, Item no. 283472.003, Textile Department, Smithsonian National Museum of American History.

[110] Michelle Hiskey, "Historic Quilt a Feather in Atlanta's Cap, <u>Atlanta Journal-Constitution</u>, Apr. 4, 1999, p. M1.

Within days, the Smithsonian Institution expressed its interest in accepting both the *Bible Quilt* and the Tree of Life appliquéd quilt as gifts. Heckman responded in a handwritten letter:

"I am most satisfied that the Smithsonian has these examples of American needlework. I doubt that there is another biblical quilt in existence, at least made under such conditions."[111]

In April 1969, Bowman wrote to Mr. and Mrs. Heckman to share with them that the *Bible Quilt* would soon be on public display at the National Museum of History and Technology for the first time. In fact, it was likely this was the first time crowds would stand in front of the *Bible Quilt* since the 1895 Cotton States and International Exposition. Bowman enclosed a copy of an article from the *Washington Post* about the quilt in her letter. She wrote:

"There has already been so much interest generated by the advance publicity about the quilt, that it seems this will be a very popular exhibit. Thank you again for your interest in adding this charming needlework to the national collection."[112]

In early June, Mr. and Mrs. Harold Heckman visited extended family in Vienna, Virginia. They also made an appointment to visit Doris Bowman at the museum. On Thursday, June 5, 1969, the couple walked into the National Museum of History and Technology, met Bowman, exchanged pleasantries, and then stood with other museum patrons to admire Powers' *Bible Quilt*.[113]

I believe accomplished woman Harriet Powers was there, too.

---

[111] Harold Heckman to Doris M. Bowman, Jan. 22, 1969, Textile Department, Smithsonian National Museum of American History.

[112] Doris M. Bowman to Mr. and Mrs. Harold M. Heckman, Apr. 9, 1969, Textile Department, Smithsonian National Museum of American History. It is likely the *Washington Post* article was from the Calendar section on April 3, 1969.

[113] Harold Heckman handwritten letter to Doris M. Bowman, May 30, 1969, Textile Department, Smithsonian National Museum of American History.

The Pictorial Quilt

The Pictorial Quilt by Harriet Powers. Athens, GA, about 1895 – 1898. Cotton plain weave, pieced, appliquéd, embroidered, and quilted. The embroidery is done with cotton and metallic yarns. Dark colored inks. Measures 68-7/8 x 105 inches. Collection Museum of Fine Arts, Boston, Bequest of Maxim Karolik, 64.619.

Quilt Block Descriptions

Harriet Powers backed the *Pictorial Quilt* with the same red plaid material shown in the binding seen on the front side. The descriptions of each block were written on postcards, which the Museum of Fine Arts acquired with the quilt.

Top Row – left to right

1. Job prays for his enemies. Two angels, Job's coffin and crosses.
2. "Black Friday" – May 19, 1780. "The cattle all went to bed, chickens to roost and the trumpet was blown. The sun went off to a small spot and then to darkness."
3. Moses with a serpent, women bringing their children for healing.
4. Adam and Eve and the Serpent in the Garden of Eden. "Adam's rib by with which Eve was made. The sun and moon. God's all seeing eye and God's merciful hand."
5. Christ is baptized by John the Baptist. A dove descends on Jesus.

Middle Row – left to right

6. Jonah thrown over the side of a boat and swallowed by a whale. Turtles swim around.
7. The creation of male and female animals.
8. Falling stars from the Leonid meteor storm, November 13, 1833.
9. More pairs of animals, including camel, elephant, giraffe, lion.
10. Angels are called by God to pour out seven vials of wrath (Revelations 15 – 16).

Bottom Row – left to right

11. Unusually heavy Georgia snowfall in February 10, 1895. "A woman frozen while at prayer. A woman frozen at a gateway. A man with a sack of meal frozen. … All blue birds killed. A man frozen at his jug of liquor."
12. Meteor showers, presumed to be from August 10 and 11, 1846. A man tolls a bell. God's hand mercifully causes no harm to the people.
13. "Bob and Kate Bell of VA," who were presumed to not know about God, share this quilt block with Betts, a hog which ran 500 miles from Georgia to Virginia.
14. More pairs of animals.
15. Jesus, with blood streaming down His right side, crucified alongside two thieves. Mary, Martha weep at the feet of Jesus.

Exhibition History

The *Pictorial Quilt* was in the possession of a private family for its first sixty-two years. Since 1960, the *Pictorial Quilt* has been on display the equivalent of 1,000 days or just under three years. While in possession of the Museum of Fine Arts, Boston, the quilt has traveled to Georgia, New York, and Ohio. Special thanks to Susan Ward, Research Fellow, Department of Textile and Fashion Arts, Museum of Fine Arts, Boston for her assistance in compiling this list.

Date	Exhibit
1898	Given to Dr. Charles Cuthbert Hall (1852—1908). At some point the *Pictorial Quilt* was displayed on a wall in Synton House, the Hall family's summer home in Westport Point, Massachusetts.
Apr. 17, 1975 – July 13, 1975	Museum of Fine Arts, Boston. The *Pictorial Quilt* is included in the exhibit "American Bed Furnishings."
June 19, 1976 – Aug. 1, 1976	Metropolitan Museum of Art, New York. On display in the "Selections of 19th Century Afro-American Art" exhibit.
Dec. 5, 1976 – Feb. 27, 1977	Atlanta Historical Society. "Missing Pieces: Georgia Folk Art 1770—1976." This is the first time in more than seventy-five years the *Pictorial Quilt* was physically back in Georgia since Harriet Powers first stitched it. The exhibit poster featured four panels from the *Pictorial Quilt*. The quilt did not continue to the other touring sites.
Feb. 1, 1978 – Apr. 2, 1978	Cleveland Museum of Art. On display in "The Afro-American Tradition in Decorative Arts" exhibit.
July 30, 1980 – Sept. 28, 1980	Museum of Fine Arts, Boston. On display in the "From Fiber to Fine Art" exhibit.

June 20, 1982 – Nov. 1, 1982	Studio Museum in Harlem, New York. On display in the exhibit "Ritual and Myth: A Survey of Afro-American Art."
Dec. 9, 1983 – Jan. 28, 1984	American Folk Art Museum, New York City. On display in the exhibit "Religious Folk Art in America: Reflections of Faith."
Feb. 13 – 24, 1987	Black History Month display in the ADA Gallery, Museum of Fine Arts, Boston.
Sept. 27, 1989 – Dec. 31, 1989	Museum of Fine Arts, Boston. On display in the exhibit "Textile Masterpieces."
Oct. 21, 1994 – Apr. 16, 1995	Museum of Fine Arts, Boston. On display in the exhibit "Sweet Dreams: Bedcovers and Bed Clothes."
Feb. 5 – 19, 1996	On special display in the American Decorative Arts Gallery, Museum of Fine Arts, Boston.
Apr. 9, 1999 – June 13, 1999	Atlanta History Center. On display in the exhibit "Georgia Quilts: Piecing Together a History." This is the second time the *Pictorial Quilt* is displayed in Georgia in a century.
Apr. 8, 2001 – Aug. 5, 2001	Museum of Fine Arts, Boston. On display in the exhibit "American Folk." The quilt did not travel to other exhibit venues.

The *Pictorial Quilt* is currently in storage at the Museum of Fine Arts and is anticipated to be on display in Fall 2010 when the museum's new American Wing opens. You can contact the museum at:

Museum of Fine Arts
465 Huntington Avenue
Boston, MA 02115-5523
(617) 267-9300, www.mfa.org

When I started this project, I wondered how I could bring anything new to the Harriet Powers story or to the collective knowledge about either of her known surviving quilts. After all, Powers herself passed away more than one hundred years ago, and her two known surviving quilts are likely the most cited quilts in quilt history.

I noticed the narrative about the *Pictorial Quilt* always mentioned Dr. Charles C. Hall, who received the *Pictorial Quilt* as a gift in 1898; his son, Rev. Basil Hall, who inherited the quilt; and an art collector named Maxim Karolik, who purchased the quilt from Rev. Hall and bequeathed it to the Museum of Fine Arts, Boston.

I wanted to know more, though. Why would these three Caucasian men be interested in *this quilt* stitched by a Black woman? Why would someone think a quilt would be an appropriate gift for Dr. Hall? What emotional attachment, if any, did Rev. Hall have for the *Pictorial Quilt* that motivated him to care for the quilt for decades? Did Maxim Karolik collect other African American artwork? Was any biographical information on these three men available?

Television police dramas call this process following the "chain of custody," where one follows the "chronological documentation, and/or paper trial, showing the seizure, custody, control, transfer, analysis, and disposition of evidence."[114]

Let's go back to the 1890s and follow where the evidence regarding the *Pictorial Quilt* leads. Let's meet a few other people, whom you've probably never heard of, who have played a part in the *Pictorial Quilt* story. Let's follow the lives, loves, and even lawsuits that point to where the *Pictorial Quilt* is today. You're sure to be surprised!

Dr. Charles Cuthbert Hall (1852—1908)

Dr. Charles Cuthbert Hall was born in New York on September 3, 1852 to William Cooper and Jane Agnes Hall. His paternal grandparents, Asahel and Elizabeth (McKenney) Hall, left England for Wallingford,

---

[114] Chain of Custody, http://en.wikipedia.org/wiki/Chain_of_custody (Accessed May 24, 2008).

Connecticut in 1800 and later moved to Albany, New York.[115] This side of the family was also related to Lyman Hall (1724—1790), who was born in Wallingford, Connecticut, and was one of the signers of the Declaration of Independence in 1776.[116] Lyman Hall also served as Governor of Georgia from 1783—1784.

Dr. Hall attended Williams College in Williamstown, Massachusetts at age sixteen. He graduated Phi Beta Kappa in 1872. He attended the Union Theological Seminary in New York from 1872 to 1874 and continued his theological studies in England and Edinburgh, Scotland. He graduated with the Union Theological Seminary, Class of 1875.

Dr. Hall married his first cousin, Jeanie Stewart Boyd, on August 2, 1877.[117] The couple had four children: Katharine Stanley Hall (1886—1970), Basil Douglas Hall (1888—1979), Eleanor MacMaster Hall (1890—1984), and Theodore Eldridge Hall (1896—1955).[118]

Ordained a Presbyterian minister, Dr. Hall served as pastor of the Union Church in Newburgh, New York from 1875 to 1877. He then served twenty years as minister of the First Presbyterian Church in Brooklyn, New York from 1877 to 1897. The First Presbyterian Church was founded in 1822. When Dr. Hall started to minister there in 1877, there were 636 members. By the time he left, its parishioners numbered 1,462.[119] Rev. Basil Hall, his son, wrote of his father:

"These two traits – the human touch and the sense of sacred mission happily blended in his personality – are among the best keys to the understanding of his prompt success.

"He was a master in the art of friendship; his life went out toward people as people, attractive or unattractive, cultured or illiterate, rich or poor, young or old. His concern for others was self-evident and of a sort to win instinctive response. To meet him

---

[115] Basil Douglas Hall, The Life of Charles Cuthbert Hall: One Among a Thousand (New York: Carlton Press, 1965), p. 13.

[116] Hall, The Life of Charles Cuthbert Hall, p. 13.

[117] Hall, The Life of Charles Cuthbert Hall, pp. 7, 16.

[118] Personal visit by author to the Dr. Charles Cuthbert Hall family plot in Westport Point, MA on May 21, 2008.

[119] Hall, The Life of Charles Cuthbert Hall, p. 93.

was to know that he cared, not in an artificial and professional way, but truly and sincerely…"[120]

The First Presbyterian Church congregation still worships today at 124 Henry Street. Rev. Cari Jackson, an African American woman, has served as Interim Senior Pastor since 2006. Like Dr. Hall, Rev. Jackson is a graduate of Union Theological Seminary.[121]

During his tenure at First Presbyterian Church, Dr. Hall also served on the Board of Trustees for Atlanta University in Georgia for a number of years until his death in 1908. Atlanta University was founded in 1865 by the American Missionary Association to educate African Americans. Rev. Basil Hall wrote that his father was a Trustee for Atlanta University from 1890 to 1908; while one historical text about the school records the tenure as 1895 to 1908.[122] At some point, Dr. Hall served as Vice President of the Board of Trustees. A memorial tribute to Dr. Hall in 1908 stated he served on the Board for thirteen years and had been the Vice President for ten years at his death.[123] Thus, it's most likely he started on the Board in 1895. Many who write about the *Pictorial Quilt* say Dr. Hall was the President of the Board of Trustees when the quilt was given to him.[124] I have not (yet) found Atlanta University records indicating Dr. Hall was ever President of the Board, though they may exist. Nor have I visited Georgia to comb through Atlanta University records or the student newspapers from the 1890s or early 1900s to confirm whether he were ever Board President.

In 1907, Dr. Hall participated in the inauguration ceremonies of his personal friend and former student, Rev. Edward Twichell Ware, as president of Atlanta University. In writing about Ware's upcoming

---

[120] Hall, The Life of Charles Cuthbert Hall, pp. 78 – 79.

[121] First Presbyterian Church website – www.FPCBrooklyn.org (accessed on May 11, 2008).

[122] Hall, The Life of Charles Cuthbert Hall, p. 7. See also Clarence A. Bacote, The Story of Atlanta University: A Century of Service 1865 – 1965 (Princeton, NJ: Princeton University Press, 1969), p. 117.

[123] "Dr. Charles Cuthbert Hall," The Bulletin Atlanta University, Apr. 1908, no. 181. Memorial article published upon his passing.

[124] Likely early researchers read that Dr. Hall was the Chairman of the Atlanta University Board of Trustees from the Museum of Fine Arts article that announced the acquisition of the *Pictorial Quilt* (Bulletin, no. 330, 1964, p. 162).

presidency, Dr. Hall provided insights into his own involvement with the school:

"As Vice President of the Board of Trustees of Atlanta University, I take pleasure in certifying that my connection with the University has extended over many years, during which I have had opportunity thoroughly to know the nature of its ideals and the character of its work. With both I find myself in sympathy. With quiet courage born of conviction Atlanta University has for more than a generation kept on its course, faithful to the purpose of its Founders. It seeks to provide an opportunity for gifted members of the colored race to have all the advantages of higher education while remaining in daily companionship with members of their own race. Thus the University accomplishes two things, it provides a succession of well trained teachers and it encourages those teachers to be products of their connection with their race, thus they go forth fitted to inspire that race with enthusiasm and self-respect."[125]

Rev. Dr. Charles Cuthbert Hall
Source: *Brooklyn Daily Eagle*, January 14, 1897

[125] Charles Cuthbert Hall, "Testimonial of Dr. Hall," The Bulletin Atlanta University, Apr. 1908, no. 181. The testimonial is dated November 30, 1907. In 1988, Atlanta University merged with Clark University. One can read the university's publications at the Robert W. Woodruff Library, Archives and Special Collections, Atlanta University Center.

Dr. Hall involved himself in the cause of African American higher education even in New York. In February 1898, for example, Dr. Hall appeared at Madison Square Garden Concert Hall where he paid tribute to the work of Samuel Chapman Armstrong (1839 – 1893), the founder of Hampton Normal and Agricultural Institute, a college for African American students. Speakers that evening also included William E. Dodge, who presided over the event, Hampton President Robert C. Ogden, Rev. Dr. H.B. Frissell, and Booker T. Washington (1856 – 1915), a Hampton graduate and leader of the Tuskegee Institute in Alabama. Washington gave a rousing speech. He said of his fellow African Americans and the need for education:

> "That a race may have a new birth – a new freedom in habits of thrift, economy, and industrial development – I take to be the meaning of this meeting....Freedom from debt, comfortable homes, profitable employment, intelligence, bring a self-respect and confidence without which no race can get on its feet. During the years of slavery we were shielded from competition. To-day, unless we prepare to complete with the outside world, we shall go to the wall as a race."[126]

The following month, March 1898, Dr. Hall appeared at the Manhattan Congregational Church with Atlanta University President Horace Bumstead and Col. George E. Waring to speak about the university. Waring recited two poems by Paul Lawrence Dunbar, apparently to the surprise of the audience.[127] Dr. Hall is quoted as saying on this occasion, "If the negro race is to be elevated, it must have negro leaders who are educated and thinking men. The life is more than meat and the body [more] than raiment."[128]

In November 1898, Dr. Hall arranged another gathering and again shared the pulpit with Atlanta University President Bumstead. They encouraged the audience, many of whom "represented to a large degree the intellectual and philanthropical elements" of New York, to support the cause of higher education for African Americans. The event was held at Brick Presbyterian Church in New York City, where Dr. Henry Van

---

[126] "Education of the Negro, The Armstrong Association Hears Speeches on the Subject from Laymen and Clergy," New York Times, Feb. 13, 1898, p. 8.

[127] "Education for Negroes," New York Times, Mar. 21, 1898. Col. Waring is George E. Waring, Jr., who was known for his work on sanitation and the American sewer system.

[128] "Education for Negroes," New York Times, Mar. 21, 1898.

Dyke, author of the Christmas story *The Other Wise Man* (1896), was pastor. For this occasion, Paul Lawrence Dunbar, "the colored poet," recited several of his own poems for the crowd.[129] Because of Dr. Hall's efforts at this event, ten donors eventually pledged $1,000 a year for two years to support Atlanta University. The $20,000 total covered the university's operating expenses for that time period.[130]

Dr. Hall was deeply religious, a teacher of theology, and a writer of hymns. Over the years, Dr. Hall wrote and published fifteen books, including *Into His Marvellous Light* (1893), *The Children, the Church and the Communion* (1895), *The Christ-filled Life* (1897), *Bible Truth in Hymns* (1899), *Christ and the Human Race* (1906), and *The Silver Cup: Simple Messages to Children* (1909).[131]

The *Pictorial Quilt* was given to Dr. Hall as a gift in 1898. By whom? For what reasons?

Dr. Gladys-Marie Fry wrote in 1976 that Harriet Powers' *Bible Quilt* "must have been seen by the wives of Atlanta University professors. These women commissioned a second narrative quilt, to be a gift in 1898 to the Reverend Charles Cuthbert Hall."[132] The wives were thought to have seen the *Bible Quilt* while it was on display at the 1895 Cotton States Exposition in Atlanta.

Was the *Pictorial Quilt* actually commissioned? Or, is it possible that Harriet Powers had completed the quilt sometime after her 1896 letter to Lorene Curtis Diver in Keokuk, Iowa when someone associated with Atlanta University approached her and she sold the completed quilt? I have found no evidence from the 1800s to support either scenario, though the evidence may exist in Atlanta University Board of Trustees records or past Atlanta University Bulletin issues.

Rev. Basil Hall mentioned, in the book he wrote about his father, that his father's story was largely constructed from personal papers, letters, diaries, and scrapbooks in the family's archives. Many of Dr. Hall's

---

[129] "Higher Education for Negroes," New York Times, Nov. 6, 1898, p. 7. See also "The Education of the Negro," New York Times, Nov. 7, 1898, p. 7.

[130] Clarence A. Bacote, The Story of Atlanta University: A Century of Service 1865 – 1965 (Atlanta: Atlanta University, 1969), p. 117 – 118. The purchasing power of the $20,000 in 2008 dollars would be $535,580, according to MeasuringWorth.com. Accessed March 1, 2009.

[131] Hall, The Life of Charles Cuthbert Hall, pp. 263 – 264 for a complete list of Dr. Hall's titles.

[132] Gladys-Marie Fry, "Harriet Powers: Portrait of a Black Quilter," in Missing Pieces: Georgia Folk Art 1770 – 1976 (Atlanta: Georgia Council for the Arts, 1976), p. 19.

papers and published writings are at the libraries of the Union Theological Seminary and Williams College. Maybe one day a researcher will locate a first-person account confirming when the *Pictorial Quilt* was given to Dr. Hall, by whom, and on what occasion.

Was the *Pictorial Quilt* actually given in 1898 or in some other year? Is there a record of Dr. Hall in Atlanta that year? Do any of the Atlanta University Board of Trustees notes, if they have survived, mention a presentation of a quilt to Dr. Hall? Why would Dr. Hall have been singled out for such a gift if he were "only" a Vice President of the Board, and not the President?

Let's assume the *Pictorial Quilt* was indeed given as a gift in 1898 to Dr. Hall. I am only speculating and have no evidence to support this thought as a fact, but what if the quilt were given to Dr. Hall as a congratulatory gift for his becoming President of the Union Theological Seminary? The *Brooklyn Eagle* newspaper reported on January 14, 1897 that Dr. Hall had been unanimously nominated as President of the Union.[133] Dr. Hall expressed surprise at the nomination and could think of no reason to leave the First Presbyterian Church. Yet, just five days later, the *Brooklyn Eagle* reported that Dr. Hall had accepted the nomination.[134] In February, Dr. Hall was unanimously elected to the presidency. He preached his last sermon at First Presbyterian Church on June 7.[135] On February 9, 1898, Dr. Hall was inaugurated at the Union Theological Seminary.[136]

Let's go back to the question of whether Harriet Powers was commissioned to make the *Pictorial Quilt* or whether she already had completed the quilt. Again, I am only speculating and have no evidence to support this thought as a fact, but could Harriet Powers have stitched the *Pictorial Quilt* between the time those in Atlanta knew about Dr. Hall's appointment as Union Theological Seminary President and one of the upcoming 1898 Atlanta University Trustees Board meetings? Be honest, if you are an experienced quilter, haven't you completed a quilt in six months or less? Maybe Powers, an accomplished quilter, did as well.

---

133 "Rev. Dr. C. C. Hall May Go," Brooklyn Eagle, Jan. 14, 1897, p. 2.

134 "Dr. Hall Accepts The Nomination for President of Union Seminary. He Makes a Statement in Which He Says Public Discussion of His Plans Is Unauthorized," Brooklyn Eagle, Jan. 19, 1897, p. 16.

135 Hall, The Life of Charles Cuthbert Hall, p. 122.

136 "Hall's Inauguration," Brooklyn Eagle, Feb. 9, 1898, p. 3.

In retrospect, an unusually designed and deeply moving quilt based on Bible stories and stitched by a former slave and accomplished, award-winning needlewoman would be quite an appropriate gift for a prominent pastor who for years championed the cause of African American education. I think Dr. Hall, Vice President of the Atlanta University Board of Trustees, would have been delighted when the *Pictorial Quilt* was presented to him, presumably on the occasion of his becoming President of the Union Theological Seminary.

I wonder. What price did Harriet Powers receive for the *Pictorial Quilt*? Was it more than the $5 she received from Jennie Smith?

I wonder. Do you think the women who organized the quilt gift would have invited Powers, who was about sixty-one years old and lived seventy miles away in the Athens, to be in attendance when the quilt was given to Dr. Hall? What would the conversation have been between forty-six-year-old Dr. Hall and Powers? Would she have shared with Dr. Hall what her inspirations were in creating each quilt block? Now, I have absolutely no evidence that Powers ever met Dr. Hall. I just wonder.

Finally, I wonder whether Mrs. Jeanie Hall, Dr. Hall's wife, kept a diary? Did she make any notes about the *Pictorial Quilt* that evening when Dr. Hall brought the piece home to her?

In 1889, Dr. Hall and his wife built a summer home in Westport Point, Massachusetts and named the home Sinton, later affectionately known as Synton House. The family had lived in houses owned by others, such as the First Presbyterian Church manse and the President's House of the Union Theological Seminary. Now the family had its own summer retreat. Rev. Hall writes of his parents and the house:

> "… they watched their house as it rose, unobstructed by the trees which now completely screen it, and in 1890, they took possession. It was large, thoroughly built by local craftsmen and very liveable. From its piazza they could watch the merchant sailing vessels passing in stately procession at sea, and the local fleet of catboats going out to the fishing grounds in the morning and returning in the afternoon…"[137]

---

[137] Hall, The Life of Charles Cuthbert Hall, p. 139.

Larry Salmon, who passed away in 1984 at the age of thirty-nine, was the Curator of Textiles at the Museum of Fine Arts, Boston from 1971 through 1980.[138] According to an October 16, 1974 note in Salmon's handwriting in the Museum of Fine Arts' *Pictorial Quilt* object file, George H. Utter, Rev. Basil Hall's son-in-law, shared that the quilt hung in the family's Westport Point, Massachusetts summer home, Synton House.

In January 1908, about ten years after receiving the *Pictorial Quilt*, Dr. Hall was struck with an "obscure disease of the liver" contracted while lecturing in India two years prior. He passed away on March 25, 1908 following a surgical procedure. He was only fifty-six years old. An honor guard of Union Theological Seminary students accompanied the family to Westport Point, where Dr. Hall was laid to rest.[139]

Rev. Basil Douglas Hall (1888—1979)

Rev. Basil Hall, Dr. Charles Hall's eldest son, was born in New York on New Year's Day 1888. He was only twenty years old and a student at Harvard University when his father became ill and unexpectedly passed away in 1908. He continued his studies and graduated from Harvard University (A.B. 1909, A.M. 1910) and the Union Theological Seminary (1912). Rev. Basil Hall married Anna Loraine Washburn in 1915. He completed Army Chaplain training school in 1918 and was commissioned chaplain with rank of First Lieutenant Officers' Reserve Corps.

Rev. Hall followed his father's profession and became a full-time minister serving churches in the Bronx, New York; Paris Hill, New York; and Florence, Massachusetts.[140] He also served a number of years as pastor of the Broad Street Christian Church in Westerly, Rhode Island.[141] His daughter, Katharine Hamlin Hall Preston, fondly remembers that her father lived a life of Christ and incorporated his religion into his life.

---

[138] "Larry Salmon was Museum's Textile Curator," Boston Globe, Dec. 10, 1984.

[139] "Dr. Charles C. Hall Dead," New York Times, Mar. 26, 1908, p. 7. See also Hall, The Life of Charles Cuthbert Hall, p. 246– 247.

[140] Katharine Hamlin Hall Preston, in-person interview with the author, May 21, 2008.

[141] The Broad Street Christian Church, originally formed in 1849, is now the location of the Granite Theatre (www.granitetheatre.com).

Preston remembers that her father wrote weekly letters to every parishioner enlisted in World War II. He once stood watch outside the home of a Japanese-American who fought for the United States in WWII when prejudiced neighbors wanted to harm the veteran and his family. In addition, Rev. Hall easily related to people. "He was a man to whom one came to for help and comfort," she shared.[142]

Rev. Hall and Anna were married more than fifty years. Preston says her mother, a Smith College graduate, was more religious than her father. "She had total faith," said Preston.[143] Anna Loraine Washburn Hall came from a prominent family. She was the great granddaughter of Cyrus Hamlin (1811—1900), an American missionary who established Roberts College in Constantinople, Turkey and served as its president (1860—1877). Cyrus Hamlin was also a cousin of Hannibal Hamlin, Vice President of the United States during the first administration of Abraham Lincoln.[144] Her father was Dr. George H. Washburn, a Tufts University professor and chair of obstetrics from 1897 to 1912.

Rev. Hall and his wife raised their family on his pastor salary. "We lived in total poverty," recalls Preston. "I never heard Mother complain. She had a wonderful life."[145]

---

[142] Katharine Hamlin Hall Preston interview, May 21, 2008.

[143] Katharine Hamlin Hall Preston interview, May 21, 2008.

[144] For a more in-depth profile of Cyrus Hamlin, visit http://library.bowdoin.edu/arch/mss/chg.shtml. Roberts College is today part of Bogazici University. For more information on the history of the two schools, visit www.boun.edu.tr/about/history.html (accessed on May 26, 2008).

[145] Katharine Hamlin Hall Preston interview, May 21, 2008.

Rev. and Mrs. Basil Hall—50th Wedding Anniversary
Photo courtesy of Mrs. Katharine Hall Preston

Rev. Hall "loved coming to Westport Point," said Preston of Synton House, the Victorian home built by Dr. Charles Cuthbert Hall. After Dr. Hall passed away, Jeanie Hall, his wife, and their daughter, Katharine Stanley Hall, and son, Theodore Eldridge Hall, lived at Synton House year-round. Mrs. Jeanie Hall was affectionately known as Baba to her grandchildren. During summers Synton House became the gathering point for extended family vacations. One of Dr. Hall's granddaughters, Janet Gillespie (1913—2005), wrote about her childhood and shared the following description of Synton House in her delightful book, <u>With a Merry Heart</u>:

> "It was a nineteenth-century "summer cottage" – a huge square house with brown shingles, a roof like a Chinese straw hat and a veranda all around, where old silvery rocking chairs sat waiting in the sun. There were enormous linden trees near one corner, and when they were in bloom the veranda and the whole house smelled of honey.

> "The view from Synton was spectacular. The sea filled the whole horizon to the south, and on the west was the tidal river running four miles inland between wooded banks. You could look

right across the Massachusetts border into Rhode Island, a feat that seemed amazing to us, but Pop told us that he could spit from Massachusetts into Rhode Island, and once he took us over to Adamsville and did it. So did we. Of course, Baba was not told of this vulgar affair."[146]

There seems to be no record of when the *Pictorial Quilt* stitched by Harriet Powers first graced the walls of Synton House. Preston remembers the quilt hanging from a wall with simple tacks. "We didn't know the quilt was special. We just loved it," she recalled.[147] The quilt hung on a wall on the second floor in a hallway that was originally part of the servants' quarters.

In April 1942, Mrs. Jeanie Hall, Dr. Charles Hall's wife, passed away and ownership of Synton House passed to the next generation.

Synton House in the 1890s
(Source: The Earliest Years at Sinton on Eldridge Heights 1888—1907
by Basil D. Hall)

---

[146] Janet Gillespie, With A Merry Heart (Boston, G. K. Hall & Co., 1977), p. 4 – 5. Gillespie was the daughter of Eleanor MacMaster Hall, the second daughter of Dr. Charles C. Hall, and the wife of Rev. Dr. Robert Russell Wicks, Dean of the Princeton University Chapel from 1928 – 1947. Janet Gillespie's other books include A Joyful Noise (NY: Harper & Row, 1971), Bedlam in the Back Seat (Westport, MA: Partners Village Press, 2001), and a gardening book.

Today one can rent the ten-bedroom Synton House on a weekly basis during the summer. Visit www.SyntonHouse.com. Can you imagine a quilting retreat at the house where Harriet Powers' *Pictorial Quilt* once hung?

[147] Katharine Hamlin Hall Preston, telephone interview with the author, March 27, 2008.

Rev. Basil Hall officiated at the weddings of his two daughters. In 1948 Anne Cuthbert Hall married George Herbert Utter, who was on staff at the *Westerly Sun* newspaper where his father, George Benjamin Utter was editor. The bridegroom's grandfather, whom he seemed to be named after, was George Herbert Utter, Governor of Rhode Island (1905—1906).[148] In 1954, Rev. Hall performed the wedding ceremony for his other daughter, Katharine Hamlin Hall, to Lieutenant John L. Preston, U.S.A.F. of Ishpeming, Michigan.[149]

In 1960, Rev. Hall was seventy-two years old. Money continued to be scarce given the upkeep of his own home in Westerly, RI and Synton House in Westport Point, MA. About 1960, George Utter, Basil Hall's son-in-law, purchased Synton House from Rev. Hall and his sister Eleanor Hall Wicks.

Robert Utter, son of Anne Hall Utter and George Utter, was born in 1953. He remembers visiting Synton House on many weekends after his father purchased the Victorian residence. Robert has fond memories of the *Pictorial Quilt*. He remembers the *Pictorial Quilt* was always there hanging on a wall in the house his great-grandfather built. He remembers being a boy about six or seven years old, playing in front of the quilt with his younger sister, Loraine, and making up stories about each quilt block as if they were pages in an illustrated book.[150] "The quilt was a living thing, not meant to be on a bed, but meant to be art—a pictorial offering," he shared in an interview at The Other Tiger, a charming, multi-room bookstore he owns in Westerly.[151]

As a child, Robert Utter did not remember the *Pictorial Quilt* leaving Synton House. "I was not aware of the quilt's disappearance until years later. Then I understood the quilt was something important. The quilt started showing up in books," he recalled.[152]

In November 1960, Rev. Hall drove to Boston with the *Pictorial Quilt* and documentation about the quilt to offer the quilt for sale to the Museum of Fine Arts. The documentation included fifteen index cards explaining each quilt block and a tiny, about 2 inches by 3 inches,

148 "G. H. Utter Marries Miss Anne C. Hall," New York Times, Aug. 1, 1948.

149 "Katharine Hall Bay State Bride," New York Times, Nov. 17, 1954.

150 Robert Utter, telephone interview with the author, Mar. 27, 2008.

151 Robert Utter, in-person interview with the author, May 22, 2008.

152 Utter interview, May 22, 2008.

photograph of Harriet Powers. The descriptions were written in an elegant handwriting. Underneath the index cards, on a separate matte board, someone else wrote in a tighter handwriting that the quilt was a gift to Dr. Charles Cuthbert Hall while he was Chairman of the Board of Trustees of Atlanta University and that the quiltmaker was a Negro woman named Mrs. Harriet Powers, born October 29, 1837. The writer goes on to say Powers was sixty years old in the photograph.[153] If Powers were indeed sixty years old, that suggests the photograph was given in 1897 or 1898, which is the timeframe when Dr. Hall is nominated and became President of the Union Theological Seminary in New York.

There does not seem to be any documentation yet found as to why Rev. Basil Hall would offer the *Pictorial Quilt* for sale to the museum given that it had been a beloved item in the family for more than sixty years. Maybe he needed the money to support his family and his older sister, Katherine Hall, who still lived at Synton House? Maybe he wanted to ensure the quilt was preserved for future generations to enjoy?

The *Pictorial Quilt* was not the only textile of significance in the Hall family. In 1965, Anna Loraine Hall, Rev. Hall's wife, donated a lace nurse's cap belonging to Florence Nightingale to the Westerly Hospital. The cap had been a family heirloom. Her great-grandfather, Cyrus Hamlin, knew Florence Nightingale during the Crimean War and supplied bread for the British troops. The cap had been a gift from Nightingale to Hamlin when she left Crimea to return to Great Britain after the war.[154] The cap remains on display today in the lobby of this Rhode Island hospital.

Once Rev. Hall took the *Pictorial Quilt* to the Museum of Fine Arts in Boston, it never returned to Synton House to grace the family's walls.

How did the art collector Maxim Karolik come to purchase the *Pictorial Quilt*? There seems to be no written record of the two men meeting in person. Karolik was a widower in 1960. He owned a home in Newport, Rhode Island, less than forty-five miles east of Westerly and about twenty-five miles south of Synton House.

---

153 Museum of Fine Arts, Boston documentation dated Nov. 2, 1960. David B. Little, Registrar.

154 Donald J. Boisvert, "Florence Nightingale's Cap," 500 Tomato Plants in the Kitchen (Xlibris Corporation, 2001), pp. 49 – 61. See also www.quahog.org/attractions/index.php?id=59 to see a photograph of the cap (accessed May 26, 2008).

Katharine Preston remembers stories of Maxim Karolik visiting elderly members of the Westport Point community to potentially purchase their antiques.[155] Had Karolik met Rev. Basil Hall on one of these antique hunts? By 1960, the *Pictorial Quilt* had been in the Hall family for six decades. For many of these years the quilt hung prominently on a wall at Synton House with simple tacks.[156] Had Karolik ever heard about the *Pictorial Quilt* from Westport Point neighbors of the Hall family?

I have no evidence to suggest that Rev. Hall ever met Karolik before November 1960. Nor have I located any diaries Karolik may have kept to see whether there were any previous meetings between the men recorded by Karolik.[157]

What was the connection between Rev. Hall and Maxim Karolik?

When I came back from a three-day research trip to Westerly, Westport Point, and Boston in May 2008, I re-read all my *Pictorial Quilt* research notes. There was a name from the 1960s that I had overlooked before that now stood out in glaring lights. Maybe that man from the 1960s could help, if he were still alive and I could find him. It took half a dozen emails to museum textile departments and public relations offices, but I learned he was still alive. With a mix of trepidation and excitement, I phoned him. He was incredibly gracious – and most likely surprised to get my telephone call. This lovely man provided the key to the connection between Rev. Hall and Karolik.

But first, let's learn about Maxim Karolik, the next owner of Harriet Powers' *Pictorial Quilt*.

---

[155] Katharine Hamlin Hall Preston interview, May 21, 2008.

[156] Mrs. Preston shared with the author how the quilt hung in Synton House. There are still visible tack holes in the *Pictorial Quilt* today. The author saw them across the top of the quilt during a visit to the Museum of Fine Arts, Boston on May 23, 2008.

[157] The author has not (yet) been able to locate any diaries of Maxim Karolik at the local private or public libraries in Newport, RI or at the Museum of Fine Arts, Boston. The late Henry Hixon Meyer was the executor of Karolik's estate. The law firm of Rackemann, Sawyer & Brewster, where he worked, is not aware of any collection, based on an October 27, 2008 telephone conversation with one prominent senior partner there.

Maxim Karolik (1893—1963)

Maxim Karolik was born a Russian Jew in Romania about 1893.[158] He was a tenor who sang with the Petrograd Opera Company, making his solo debut in 1917. In 1924, when he was thirty years old, Maxim Karolik immigrated to the United States. For a short time, he lived in Illinois and sang with the Chicago Opera Company as a concert tenor.[159] In December 1927, he made his New York debut.

In addition to singing in concert halls, Karolik performed in homes of the wealthy. He ultimately made his base in Washington, D.C. In 1927, he met Martha Catharine Codman, an unmarried socialite, who hired him to give a recital in her Washington, D.C. home for forty invited guests, including the Belgian Ambassador and Baroness de Cartier, British Ambassador Sir Henry Getty Chilton and Lady Katharine Chilton, and author Mrs. Maude Howe Elliott, who wrote a book about women's art at the 1893 Chicago World's Fair.[160]

Miss Codman, as she was referred to in the society pages, could trace her family in the United States back to the early 1700s. She was the great-great-granddaughter of Elias Haskett Derby (1739—1799), a Salem, Massachusetts shipping magnate who was among the first Americans to trade directly with China and among the first Americans to achieve millionaire status.[161] Martha's father was painter John Amory Codman (1824—1886). He specialized in capturing seascapes, landscapes and portraits in oil and watercolor. Several of his works survive today at the Museum of Fine Arts, Boston.

John and his wife, Martha Pickman Rogers Codman, married in 1850, lived in Boston and had two children. Their son, John Jr., died in 1876 at the age of twenty-five. Their daughter, who was also named Martha, was born on July 24, 1858.

---

[158] Ancestry.com. New York Passenger Lists, 1820-1957 [database on-line]. Provo, UT, USA: The Generations Network, Inc., 2006. Original data: Passenger and Crew Lists of Vessels Arriving at New York, New York, 1897-1957.

[159] "News of Chicago Society," Chicago Daily Tribune, Jan. 3, 1932, p. F2. See also "New Casino to Be Reproduction," Chicago Daily Tribune, Mar. 1, 1928, p. 31.

[160] "Capital Society Events," Washington Post, Mar. 8, 1927, p. 7.

[161] Wikipedia contributors, "Elias Hasket Derby," Wikipedia, The Free Encyclopedia, http://en.wikipedia.org/w/index.php?title=Elias_Hasket_Derby&oldid=226845827 (accessed August 1, 2008).

Four days after John Amory Codman's death on December 13, 1886, marital scandal visited the family when his will, dated 1880, was filed and made public. Codman, who died at sixty-two years old with an estate valued at $400,000, apparently provided for his mistress far better than his wife in his will.[162]

Mrs. Codman and her twenty-nine-year-old daughter Martha contested John Codman's last will and testament. They asserted his mistress of fourteen years, Mrs. Eliza Ann Hales "Violet" Kimball, a widow "in the neighborhood of 45" years old, was not eligible to any provision in the will. The suit stated that Mrs. Kimball "having great influences over [Mr. Codman], she wrongfully induced him to make the bequests in her favor. It is also claimed that the deceased was of unsound mind at the time of making the will..."[163]

Details of Codman's will and affair with Violet Kimball would soon be widely reported in Boston, New York, and Washington, D.C. newspapers.

In May 1887, the Suffolk County Probate Court was filled with people hoping to hear details about the case. One day in particular stood out. During the trial, stunning new evidence surfaced. Love letters discovered inside "an old leather valise ... found among the effects of Mr. Codman" were entered into evidence.[164] News reports said there were 1,900 love letters from Kimball to Codman.[165] On May 17, the entire day was spent reading selected, "spicy" letters in open court.

In July, Judge McKim rendered his decision. He proclaimed that John Codman was of sound mind and not under undue influence when he wrote his will. As a result, the 1880 will stood. Mrs. Codman would receive $5,000 and Violet Kimball would get $40,000. As for the rest, the *New York Times* reported:

> "The balance of the estate, estimated at $348,000, is divided
> into two parts – one half being held in trust for Mrs. Codman

162 "Codman Family Scandal: The Wild Rich Man's Will Offered for Probate," Boston Daily Globe, Mar. 23, 1887. The purchasing power of the $400,000 estate in 2008 dollars would be $9.4 million, according to MeasuringWorth.com.

163 "Codman Family Scandal," Boston Daily Globe, Mar. 23, 1887. See also "Mrs. Kimball's Love Letters," New York Times, June 29, 1887, p. 1.

164 "Love Letters in Court," New York Times, May 18, 1887.

165 "Violet's Picture: Identified by the Widow of John Amory Codman," Boston Daily, Dec. 14, 1887.

during her life and the other half in trust for Miss Codman during her life. It is also provided that in certain contingencies Mrs. Kimball is to receive the income of portions of the property left to Mrs. and Miss Codman, so that it is possible that she [Mrs. Kimball] may receive, in addition to the $40,000 and $13,000 in notes also given in the will, the income of $300,000."[166]

After the court's pronouncement, the *New York Times* reporter wrote: "But Mrs. Codman, it is believed, will never yield the field to her husband's lover until the court of last resort decides against her, and a trial in the Supreme Court that will elevate the roofs of several Beacon Hill households may be expected."[167]

Within a week, Mrs. Codman and her daughter filed an appeal suggesting fourteen reasons the Supreme Court of Massachusetts should set aside the lower court's decision.[168] The appeal was heard by a jury. Newspapers speculated whether Kimball would appear in court to face Mrs. and Miss Codman and testify. As one reporter put it, "The court room was crowded to the limit of comfort with an eager audience, drawn thither by curiosity to look upon the woman whose personal charms were so potent a factor in the disposal of the Codman estate."[169]

During the proceedings, the jury heard about John Codman's heavy drinking (rum and water) and cigar smoking, especially in the years before his death. A veteran police officer testified to twice finding Codman outside in the early morning hours seemingly afraid of potential burglars in his home, though the policeman found no evidence of any.[170] A tearful Mrs. Codman testified to troubling details about her husband, including that he "frequently expressed a fear that he would die, like his mother, of softening of the brain." She also testified that Codman's "interest in his own business affairs grew less from year to year, and the care of the family estate fell largely upon" Mrs. Codman.[171] The *Washington Post* reported on its front page that when Mrs. Codman

---

166 "The Codman Will Stands," New York Times, July 10, 1887.

167 "The Codman Will Stands," New York Times, July 10, 1887.

168 "The Codman Will Case," New York Times, July 15, 1887. See also "Have Not Given Up Hope," Boston Daily Globe, July 14, 1887, p. 5 for the specific fourteen reasons.

169 "Violet's Picture," Boston Daily, Dec. 14, 1887, p.4, included a drawing of Kimball, who did not show in court that day.

170 "An Angel in Trousers," Boston Daily Globe, Dec. 20, 1887.

171 "Violet's Picture," Boston Daily, Dec. 14, 1887, p. 4.

concluded her testimony, "nearly every woman in the court-house was crying."[172]

In December 1887, after eight hours of jury deliberations, the Court reversed the lower court's decision and found that Violet Kimball indeed did exert undue influence on John Codman in the creation of the 1880 will.[173] Codman's previous will, dated 1872, would now stand.

Unbelievably, the will dated 1872 again gave very favorable terms to Violet Kimball, Codman's mistress of fourteen years.[174] Mrs. Codman, as resolute as ever, continued her legal battle to preserve the family's estate for herself and her sole surviving child, Martha.

In January 1889, three years after John Codman's death, the Supreme Judicial Court of Massachusetts finally announced a settlement. Violet Kimball would receive only $15,000. She would also sign a release relinquishing all claims on the estate of John Amory Codman. The balance of the estate, after a few specific monetary gifts and court costs, would go "absolutely to Mrs. and Miss Codman."[175]

The Codman wealth was retained in the family because of the steely determination of mother and daughter. We'll never know what would have happened if the Codman wealth had been legally passed to Violet Kimball. It's not too outrageous to believe Maxim Karolik might not have purchased the *Pictorial Quilt* if the Codman riches went to Violet Kimball, as we'll see.

Mrs. John Amory Codman died six years later in February 1905.

Miss Codman left Boston after her mother's passing to take up residence in the nation's capital. Her cousin, Ogden Codman, Jr. (1863—1951), an architect and interior designer, built her a four-story, forty-room red brick house with an Italian terrace garden at 2145 Decatur Place, NW in Washington, D.C.[176] Ogden Codman also designed a

---

172 "A Big Boston Sensation," Washington Post, Dec. 15, 1887, p. 1.

173 "Twelve Wise Men Say," Boston Daily Globe, Dec. 25, 1887, p. 5. See also "The Codman Will Case: Mrs. Violette Kimball Found Guilty of Fraud by the Jury," Washington Post, Dec. 25, 1887, p. 4.

174 "Another Will of Mr. Codman," New York Times, Jan. 16, 1889, p. 1.

175 "Violet's $15,000," Boston Daily Globe, Apr. 20, 1889. Also Supreme Judicial Court of MA, William S. Dexter, executor, v. Martha P.R. Codman & another. 148 Mass. 421; 19 N.W. 517.

176 The Codman-Davis House still stands today. It's on the National Register of Historic Places. See also "Build Costly Homes: People of Wealth Select This City as Place to Live," Washington Post, May 31, 1906. The article says the Codman house costs $80,000 to build.

twenty-four room summer mansion on Bellevue Avenue and East Bowery Street in Newport, Rhode Island called "Berkeley Villa" for Martha Codman in 1910. Newport held pleasant memories for Martha. Her family spent summers there and purchased the land on which Berkeley Villa would stand.[177]

In July 1927, Martha Codman hosted a musical recital at Berkeley Villa for the Newport summer crowd. Two hundred invited guests listened to a concert performed by the tenor Maxim Karolik, who previously performed at her D.C. mansion, and Sergei Kotiarsky, a violin soloist from the Philadelphia Symphony.[178]

A deep friendship and then romance blossomed between Maxim Karolik, who had been in the United States for just four years, and Martha Codman, whose family had been in the United States for more than four generations.

By now, Martha's fortune was estimated at $5 million by one source and between $25 million and $40 million by another source.[179] Family members and friends were concerned that Karolik was taking advantage of the millionairess. One of Karolik's friends, pianist and composer Nicolas Slonimsky, wrote in his autobiography that the "Codman clan" hired detectives to learn more about Karolik, but that the detectives found him to be "without blemish."[180] Martha would surely be sensitive to someone trying to take advantage of her wealth given the very public three-year legal fight she and her mother waged to protect the family's fortune. Besides her money, family and friends were concerned for one other reason.

Despite gossips and detectives lurking in the background, Karolik publicly denied any plans to marry Miss Codman.[181] Yet privately, Martha wrote to her aunt, Mrs. Arthur Amory (Mary) Codman:

---

[177] "Mrs. Karolik, 92 Art Patron, Dies," New York Times, Apr. 22, 1948. Martha Karolik actually died at age 89. She was born on July 24, 1858. Many newspapers mistakenly printed 92.

[178] "Miss Codman Gives a Large Musicale," New York Times, July 22, 1927.

[179] "Boston's Golden Maxim," Time, Dec. 22, 1941. Time provided the $5m estimate. The "purchasing power" of $5 million in 1928 would be $62.8 million in 2008, according to MeasuringWorth.com. The New York Times ("Maxim Karolik Art Patron, Dies," Dec. 21, 1963) estimated Codman's net worth at the time of her marriage at between $25m - $40m.

[180] Slonimsky, Nicolas, Perfect Pitch (NY: Oxford University Press, 1988), p. 109.

[181] "Maxim Karolik Dies: A Patron of the Arts," Newport Daily News, Dec. 21, 1963.

"Now I am going to tell you an important piece of news – I expect to be married in a few weeks and I think it is my Duty, as well as my pleasure to let you know beforehand, although I am keeping it a secret until after the Ceremony, because of the American papers …. The man is a Russian named Maxim Karolik, I met him in Washington a year ago…. He was at my house almost every day, and when I went to Newport, he was my guest all summer…. Having lived under my roof for more than five months, I can say that I know him thoroughly…. He is a gentleman to his fingertips, has a wonderful mind, a lovely disposition, and is a splendid singer…. Of course I know what people will say – but I am determined not to pay any attention to that, but get all the happiness and pleasure out of what remains to me of life – no matter what they think or say – they will, I am sure gladly come to my dinners, and musical entertainments."[182]

Martha's attorney, John R. Lazenby, announced the marriage of Codman, who was just months shy of her seventieth birthday, to Maxim Karolik, who was only thirty-five years old. The age difference, which raised the eyebrows of many friends and family, did not bother the couple. They exchanged their wedding vows on the French Riviera on February 2, 1928.[183]

In addition to a love of music, the couple shared a love of art. Martha Codman Karolik had been collecting eighteenth century furniture and other art objects for a number of years before meeting Maxim Karolik. About 1935, the couple decided to build its collection "in collaboration with the Boston Museum of Fine Arts."[184]

In 1939 the couple donated about 275 engravings, furniture, silver, paintings, and needlework objects made from 1720 to 1820. The collection was formally named the M. and M. Karolik Collection of Eighteenth-Century American Arts and was valued at $400,000 when it was donated.[185] A massive 366-page catalog featuring photos of the items was published in 1941.

---

[182] Martha Codman to Mrs. Arthur Codman, 30 Dec. 1927, Codman Papers, Massachusetts Historical Society, Boston. In "The Incomparable Max," American Art, Summer 1993, pp. 66 – 67.

[183] "Martha C. Codman Is Married in France," New York Times, Feb. 16, 1928.

[184] "The American Way: A Conversation Piece," The Atlanta Monthly, Oct. 1942.

[185] "Boston Museum Gets 18th Century Art," New York Times, Jan. 23, 1939.

Martha and Maxim Karolik, after the first collection, focused on acquiring early (pre-Civil War) American paintings for the benefit of the Museum of Fine Arts. They made an extraordinary arrangement with the museum. "…Karolik would do most of the shopping, the curators had the right to refuse any painting he proposed for the collection, and although he would write the checks, the objects themselves would never be owned by the Karoliks but would come directly to the museum."[186] The first year Maxim Karolik started the couple's second collection, he purchased "68 paintings…at an average of around $750 apiece."[187]

The Karoliks eventually donated a collection of 225 paintings to the Museum of Fine Arts in 1945. The gift's formal name was the M. and M. Karolik Collection of American Paintings 1815—1865.

In 1948, after a year's illness, Martha Codman Karolik passed away in her Newport, Rhode Island home at the age of eighty-nine. The couple had celebrated their twentieth wedding anniversary just two months earlier. Maxim Karolik was said to be "disconsolate" when his wife died.[188] He said of his wife in one interview:

"It was the most wonderful thing that ever happened [their marriage]… I had lived just for myself… Then I realized that Martha loved me, and it was like coming from a world of darkness into eternal light.

"Martha had so much. She possessed culture, understanding, sympathy, all the finest traits that a person can possess. She was a great soul and just by being near her I seemed to acquire some of her best qualities.

"… Martha used to say that to feel better one might need only a good steak, but to feel finer something more than that was needed…We wanted to give that 'something' to the people. Martha was always that way. She was truly a wonderful woman. I miss her so much."[189]

---

[186] Carol Troyen. "Maxim and Martha Karolik – Boston's Legendary Patrons of American Art," Architectural Digest, Dec. 1992, p. 78.

[187] John Russell. "Boston Collectors Who Applied Themselves to the Public Good," New York Times, Apr. 14, 1985.

[188] Slonimsky, Perfect Pitch, p. 110.

[189] Watson Crews, Jr., "Romantic Refugee's $25,000,000 Legacy," American Weekly, Aug. 6, 1948, p. 5.

Martha bequeathed to the Museum of Fine Arts all artwork of hers at the museum at the time of her death. Everything else she gave to Karolik, her "beloved husband and friend."[190] One report estimated she died with an estate valued at $25 million.[191] Regardless of the amount, it's not too outrageous to believe that the Museum of Fine Arts and the American public would not have the benefit of the M. and M. Karolik Collections if Martha and her mother had not fought so hard to retain the Codman wealth in the late 1890s.

In May 1958, the Museum of Fine Arts appointed Maxim Karolik an honorary curator of American Arts in appreciation of his nearly twenty-five year association with the institution.[192]

Karolik continued to collect art for the public's benefit. In 1962, he donated the M. and M. Karolik Collection of Water Colors and Drawings 1800—1875 to the Museum of Fine Arts. Then *New York Times* art critic Brian O'Doherty said of the Collections: "It is generally agreed that the three Karolik collections compose the most important single collection of 18th century and 19th century American art in any museum."[193]

Karolik continued to live in Berkeley Villa, the Newport home he shared with Martha, though he spent the winters in Boston at the Ritz-Carlton on Arlington Street and Newberry.[194] One noted summer guest to Berkeley Villa was Jacqueline Kennedy. She came occasionally for tea with Karolik and to ask his opinions about the White House restorations she was undertaking. Karolik shared with one reporter that his household staff was shocked that the First Lady "came so informally in a station wagon and left the secret service men outside the gate."[195] Karolik

---

[190] Will of Martha Catharine Karolik, Newport, RI, May 7, 1946.

[191] Crews, American Weekly, Aug. 6, 1948, p. 5.

[192] "Maxim Karolik Dies; A Patron of the Arts," Newport Daily News, Dec. 21, 1963.

[193] Brian O'Doherty, "Art: Third Karolik Collection in Boston," New York Times, Oct. 18, 1962.

[194] Alison Arnold, "The Story Behind an Art Legacy," Boston Sunday Globe, Aug. 31, 1975. Berkeley Villa stands today on Bellevue Avenue in Newport, RI. The house is sometimes referred to as the Karolik House or the Bellevue House. See also "The House of Worth" by Christopher Mason, New York Times, Feb. 16, 2006 for article and lovely photographs of the restoration to the home by its owner, Ronald Lee Fleming.

[195] Marjorie Mills, "Karolik Collection on Block," Boston Herald, June 10, 1964.

eventually donated a nineteenth-century mahogany library table to the White House restoration efforts.[196]

Maxim Karolik

Why would Karolik, an expert in nineteenth-century art, be interested in a quilt made by a former slave? Karolik was, by many accounts, self-assured and gregarious. *New York Times* art critic Brian O'Doherty wrote of Karolik:

"He is a large, handsome, voluble, impossible man, with a fine head set on slightly hunched shoulders, a strong aquiline nose, hooded eyes, and large masculine ears. Two deep wrinkles place brackets around his wide mouth, and indeed around everything that comes out of it, for he is continually quoting authority which most frequently turns out to be himself."[197]

---

[196] Marjorie Hunter, "Mrs. Kennedy Shows New Look of Old White House Library," New York Times, June 22, 1962.

[197] Brian O'Doherty, Maxim Karolik 1893 – 1963 (Boston: Museum of Fine Arts, 1963), p. 1.

Karolik may have been a character, but he had definite opinions on "good" art. In 1945, he wrote about the philosophy he and his wife shared when collecting pieces:

> "We discarded the motto of the fashionable connoisseur: "Tell me who the painter is and I will tell you whether the painting is good." Our motto was: "Tell me whether the painting is good and I will not care who the painter is."

> "People who would like to see representative works by the well-known and much-praised painters will find them in this collection; but they are incidental to a larger purpose, which is to tell the whole story through that period – the story of the known, the little known, and the unknown artists. Only an ensemble of all types of creative work, I believe, can adequately show what happened in that period. The well-known names – the popular Stars – are only part of the story."[198]

By his own words, Maxim Karolik's openness to artwork by unknown artists would have made him receptive to a piece by an unknown former slave named Harriet Powers. While Powers' name is revered today, in January 1961 when Karolik first saw her *Pictorial Quilt*, she was known primarily to the Hall family and her own family and friends in Athens, Georgia. Even the *Bible Quilt,* now at the Smithsonian National Museum of American History, was still in the private hands of Harold M. Heckman, the executor of Jennie Smith's estate, in Athens.

Was the *Pictorial Quilt* the only textile in the M. and M. Karolik Collections? No. The first collection, the one covering artwork from 1720—1820, included several needlework pieces. One needlework panel in silk, ca. 1740 from Salem, Massachusetts, depicts a French scene where a young man kisses his bride, while his African servant waits at his side.[199] Love Rawlins Pickman (1732—1809) embroidered the piece, *The Kiss Returned*, and three others in the Collection.

---

[198] M. and M. Karolik Collection of American Paintings, 1815 to 1865 (Cambridge: Published for Museum of Fine Arts, Boston [by] Harvard University Press, 1949), pp. ix, x.

[199] Eighteenth Century American Arts: The M. and M. Karolik Collection (Cambridge: Published for Museum of Fine Arts, Boston [by] Harvard University Press, 1941), pp. 273 – 274. Accession no. 39.240. See also no. 39.239.

Was the *Pictorial Quilt* the only artwork in the Karolik Collections to provide insight into aspects of African American culture? No.

There are more than three thousand pieces in the combined Karolik Collections today. While it may exist, I have not been able to locate any journal article or academic paper that deals exclusively with African American imagery in the M. and M. Karolik Collections. Nor have I found any articles that may shed light on Karolik's feelings about U.S. race relations, though these may exist.

I was able to locate eighteen paintings and drawings with definite or likely African American imagery in the collective M. and M. Karolik Collections, though there may be additional ones.[200] They are:

James Goodwyn Clonney (1812—867)
- *Corner Shop* (1830–1867): A graphite and wash painting of a man speaking to a young (possibly) African American shop boy outside some type of store or shoe shine stand. No. 1972.732.
- *In the Woodshed* (1838): A Black man with a pipe is talking with a white man in a woodshed. No. 47.1193. See also study drawing No. 48.496.
- *In the Cornfield* (1844): A young Black man sits on a horse while talking with a young white man. No. 47.1263.
- Study for *Dancing on a Stone Boat*: Central Figure (1845): A Black man looks over left shoulder while dancing a jig. No. 60.994a.
- Study for *Militia Training*: Boy Dancing (1839): Black boy dances gently while holding a hat in his left hand. No. 62.215.
- *Waking Up* (1851): A sleeping Black man with a fishing pole in one hand is about to be awakened by two young, white mischievous boys. No. 47.1189.
- *What a Catch!* (1855): A Black man stands up in a fishing boat enthusiastically waving his catch. Three other men are in the boat as well. No. 47.1217. See also study sketches: No. 48.422 and No. 52.1577.

---

[200] To see a photograph of any painting on the list, visit the Museum of Fine Arts, Boston website at www.mfa.org. Type in the title or accession number of the item in the website's search box. You can even send a free electronic postcard of the painting to someone from the museum's website.

John Mackie Falconer (1820—1903)
- *Young Man in White Apron* (probably 1851): A tired young Black man rests on what seems to be an ice block. No. 59.102.

Henry Inman (1801—1846)
- *Dismissal of School on an October Afternoon* (1845): An elderly Black man observes a dozen schoolchildren leaving class at the end of the day. No. 48.432.

Louis Maurer (1832—1932)
- *A Hot Race From the Start* (unknown): Nine jockeys urge their horses forward. The second jockey appears to be a man of color. No. 51.2532.

Samuel Finley Breese Morse (1791—1872)
- *The Boy and the Owl* (unknown): A young Black boy, sitting in a rowboat and wearing a straw hat, peers curiously at an owl perched on a nearby tree branch. The painting is attributed to Morse, though it might actually be by another painter. No. 61.304.

William Sidney Mount (1807—1868)
- *Rustic Dance After a Sleigh Ride* (1830): A Black man plays the violin for two dancing couples in a room filled with guests. Two young Black men, probably servants, observe from different locations behind the crowd. No. 48.458.
- *The Bone Player* (1856): Portrait of a handsome, lively bone player musician, who wears gold earrings. No. 48.461.

Thomas Nast (1840—1902)
- *Entrance of the Fifty-Fifth Massachusetts (Colored) Regiment Into Charleston, S.C., Feb. 21, 1865* (1865): Jubilant celebration as African American soldiers march down a street with cheering Black men, women, and children looking on. No. 59.940.

David Hunter Strother/ "Porte Crayon" (1816—1888)
- *Cotton Depot on the Bluff at the Memphis Landing, Tennessee* (1862): Dozens and dozens of cotton bales await loading on either horse-drawn carts or on waiting boats in the nearby river. In the foreground of the picture, four Black men appear to be resting and talking. No. 55.871.

C. Winter (1820s—1860s?)
- *Minstrel Show* (1850s): Seven men are dancing in black face on a Philadelphia stage. No. 48.493.

Unknown Artist
- *A Negro* (19th century): A Black man faces the viewer while wearing a three-quarter-length jacket. The drawing is made of black chalk on yellow paper. No. 61.254.

William Matthew Prior (1806—1873)
- *Three Sisters of the Copeland Family* (1854): Portrait of Eliza, Nellie, and Margaret Copeland of Boston. No. 48.467.

In 1954, Maxim Karolik purchased at least two additional William Matthew Prior paintings with African American imagery. These are the gorgeous portraits of *Nancy Lawson* (1843) and *William Lawson* (1843) now at the Shelburne Museum in Shelburne, Vermont.[201]

Do the M. and M. Karolik Collections include any nineteenth-century artwork created by African Americans? The artists listed above were born in places as varied as Edinburgh, Scotland; Biebrich-on-the-Rhine, Germany; New York; Pennsylvania; and Maine. From biographical sketches of the artists listed above, none appears to be African American. In my research, I located only one Black artist represented in the M. and M. Karolik Collections—Harriet Powers.[202]

Powers' *Pictorial Quilt* is usually placed in the context of other quilts, textiles, or folk art. I was surprised to learn the *Pictorial Quilt* and the powerful, positive family imagery of William Matthew Prior's *Three Sisters of the Copeland Family* were actually part of the same Collection and purchased by the same art collector, Maxim Karolik.

---

[201] Carol Troyen, "Maxim Karolik," <u>Antiques</u>, Apr. 2001, p. 592. Separately, the Shelburne Museum has a collection of more than 400 American quilts made in the eighteenth and nineteenth centuries.

[202] The Museum of Fine Arts, Boston has a collection of about seventy quilts. The only other quilt by an African American in the collection is by Faith Ringgold (accession no. 1991.625), according to a March 4, 2009 email to the author from the museum.

William Matthew Prior (1806—1873), *Three Sisters of the Copeland Family,* 1854, 26 7/8 x 36 1/2 inches, Bequest of Martha C Karolik for the M. and M. Karolik Collection of American Paintings, 1815-1865, Museum of Fine Arts, Boston, No. 48.467.

By 1960 the M. and M. Karolik Collections, one of the most important art collections in the United States at the time, did not include a single art object made by an African American. So how did the art collector Maxim Karolik come to purchase the *Pictorial Quilt*? Were Rev. Basil Hall, whose family owned the quilt for six decades, and Maxim Karolik acquainted? Who was the incredibly gracious man who provided the key to this mystery when I telephoned him?

On Wednesday, November 2, 1960, Rev. Basil Hall took the *Pictorial Quit,* the note cards with the quilt descriptions, and photo of Powers to the Museum of Fine Arts in Boston.

"A man walked in one day and put it on the table," said Adolph S. Cavallo, the Textile Curator at the Museum of Fine Arts in 1960 and the gracious person who shared with me his recollections of the *Pictorial*

Quilt.[203] "He was soft-spoken, pleasant, and agreeable." The man was Rev. Basil Hall.

"I had never seen a quilt like that," Cavallo recalled. "The richness of her [Harriet Powers'] imagination was fascinating, so touching, so sweet, and so human. Even the Crucifixion [block] had a great deal of feeling."

That afternoon, Rev. Basil Hall offered to sell the *Pictorial Quilt* to the museum. He must have shared with Cavallo the story of how the *Pictorial Quilt* came to be a family treasure. He might even have shared how the quilt had been displayed in Synton House. Rev. Hall might have smoothed his hands over the blocks of Bible stories one last time before he signed the necessary paperwork confirming he was offering to sell Harriet Powers' quilt and documentation to the museum and stating he was leaving the items with the museum while it considered the purchase.[204] Rev. Hall traveled back home without the beloved family quilt, which had been given to his father, Dr. Charles Cuthbert Hall, in 1898.

Later Cavallo asked Carl Zahn, the museum's Publications Director, to see the quilt and remembered Zahn thought the *Pictorial Quilt* block designs reminded him of the French artist Henri Matisse.

"The quilt looked like it could have been done in the 1970s," said Carl Zahn, now retired from the museum. "It reminded me of the works of Paul Rant or Henri Matisse in his later years."[205]

On January 12, 1961, about ten weeks after leaving the *Pictorial Quilt* with the museum, Rev. Hall contacted Cavallo to see whether any purchase decision had been made. Rev. Hall wrote, "I imagine your silence probably means that the Museum does not find it of much value. We do not want to burden you with its care, for you have already been most generous in keeping it."[206] Rev. Hall went on to mention that he and his wife will be available to pick up the quilt at a convenient time.

---

203 Adolph S. Cavallo, telephone interview with the author, May 26, 2008.

204 Document offering an appliqué quilt and framed commentary for sale to the Museum by Basil D. Hall of Westport Point, MA, November 2, 1960. David B. Little, Registrar. *Pictorial Quilt* file, Textile Department, Museum of Fine Arts, Boston.

205 Carl Zahn, telephone interview with the author, Sept. 11, 2008.

206 Basil D. Hall to Adolph Cavallo, January 12, 1961, Karolik-Codman Family Papers, Massachusetts Historical Society.

Cavallo knew the Textile Department could afford to purchase the *Pictorial Quilt* from Rev. Basil Hall. However, he felt the quilt would gain more prestige if it were part of the M. and M. Karolik Collections. Cavallo suspected that Maxim Karolik, whom he always liked, would also personally be interested in the quilt.[207]

"He was sensitive and had a sense for folk art," Cavallo explained.

On Wednesday, January 18, 1961 Karolik visited the museum to see the quilt.

"When Maxim Karolik saw the quilt," Cavallo said, "he was absolutely charmed." Karolik readily agreed to acquire the *Pictorial Quilt* from Rev. Basil Hall for the Museum of Fine Arts.

Mrs. Katherine Preston, one of Rev. Hall's daughters, thought the quilt was purchased for $800.[208] A note dated October 16, 1974 in the handwriting of Larry Salmon, then Director of Textiles at the museum, summarized a conversation between himself and George H. Utter, a son-in-law of Rev. Hall. Utter suggested the quilt was sold to Karolik for $250.[209]

Karolik, who by now had a twenty-five year relationship with the museum, wrote to Rev. Hall immediately:

> "Yesterday I was at the Museum of Fine Arts and Mr. Cavallo showed me your quilted bed cover. It is charming. He didn't know what it is worth. I said to him that I am ready to pay five hundred dollars ($500.00) for it. He advised me to write to you direct. If the above mentioned sum of five hundred dollars is acceptable to you, then I am inclined to acquire it."[210]

---

[207] Cavallo interview, May 26, 2008.

[208] Katharine Hamlin Hall Preston, telephone interview with the author, Mar. 27, 2008. MeasuringWorth.com suggests the "purchasing power" of $800 in 1961 would be $5,757 in 2008.

[209] Personal communication, Mr. George H. Utter to Larry Salmon (MFA, Boston), Oct. 16, 1974, in Textile Department files, Museum of Fine Arts, Boston. The purchasing power of $250 in 1961 would be $1,799 in 2008 dollars, according to MeasuringWorth.com. In 1974, Rev. Basil Hall was 86 years old. It is unclear why there would have been any conversation between Mr. Utter and Mr. Salmon 13 years after the *Pictorial Quilt* was sold by Rev. Basil Hall. It is only my speculation, I have no evidence of this, but perhaps the conversation was motivated by the MFA exhibit, *American Bed Furnishing*, which opened in April 1975. The *Pictorial Quilt* was a featured item.

[210] Maxim Karolik to Basil D. Hall, January 19, 1961, Karolik-Codman Family Papers, Massachusetts Historical Society. MeasuringWorth.com suggests the purchasing power of $500 in 1961 would be $3,597.98 in 2008.

Karolik was going to be traveling for several weeks and asked Rev. Hall to contact Cavallo if the price was acceptable.

On Sunday, January 22, 1961, Rev. Hall wrote to Cavallo:

"I have just received a letter from Mr. Karolik...in which he tells me that he is inclined to acquired our old quilted bed cover and that he is prepared to offer five hundred dollars ($500.00) for its purchase...Mrs. Hall and I want to assure you that we feel this offer to be most generous. We shall be grateful to you if you will thus inform Mr. Karolik...

"It will be good for us to realize that this old treasure will be safely guarded into the future and available to students of American folklore. We are surprised, I confess, that it met with such cordial reception among experts, like yourself, in these matters, although we had felt that it was unusual and that it deserved closer study before we stored it away privately."[211]

Oh, to see how close the *Pictorial Quilt* came from being withdrawn and kept within the Hall family private collection!

The *Pictorial Quilt* physically stayed at the Museum of Fine Arts after Karolik purchased it. Maxim Karolik never took possession of the quilt or displayed it in his own home per the agreement Maxim and Martha Karolik made decades prior with the museum.

On December 10, 1963, Karolik visited the Museum of Fine Arts for a photographic shoot. Brian O'Doherty was working on a formal biographical sketch of Karolik for the museum. Carl Zahn invited famed, local photographer Steven Trefonides to create the images for the sketch. The outcome of the photo shoot was incredible. The sharp black and white photographs seem to capture the very essence of Karolik's personality and spirit.[212]

The following week Maxim Karolik traveled to New York City to work on arrangements for art lectures he would give there. Sadly, he had

[211] Basil D. Hall to Adolph Cavallo, January 22, 1961, Karolik-Codman Family Papers, Massachusetts Historical Society. A note in the *Pictorial Quilt* file at the Museum of Fine Arts, Boston Textile Department indicated the quilt was sold to Karolik and transferred to the Museum on February 7, 1961.

[212] Actual photographic prints are included in what became a memorial book, Maxim Karolik (1893 – 1963), by Brian O'Doherty (Boston, Museum of Fine Arts, 1963).

a heart attack and passed away five days before Christmas at the age of seventy.[213] In his will, Karolik directed specific monetary gifts be given to selected persons on behalf of his wife, Martha, and to selected family members who survived him. He willed the remainder of his estate to the Museum of Fine Arts, Boston for the benefit of the Paintings and Prints departments.[214]

The *Pictorial Quilt* and documentation were formally offered to the museum in May 1964, along with several hundred items from Karolik's estate. Cavallo recommended the Museum accept the bequest by writing:

> "This textile has great charm and character. It is an eminently publishable piece, not only because of the bold, simple character of the pattern, but also because of the sincerely naïve yet deep sentiments expressed by the maker in … hand-written cards carrying the explanation of the scenes."[215]

The *Pictorial Quilt*, now sixty-six years old, had a new home.

One of the curious aspects of the *Pictorial Quilt* is its inconsistent design and construction of the eyes on animals in several of the blocks. Despite the *Pictorial Quilt* being arguably the most cited and published quilt in American quilt history, no one seems to have mentioned this inconsistency in the animal eyes. Art historian Dr. Regenia A. Perry's large format book on Harriet Powers provides one of the best close-up photos of the *Pictorial Quilt* and *Bible Quilt*.

In the *Bible Quilt*, Harriet Powers appliquéd eyes onto several of the animals. No human figure had appliquéd or needlework eyes, except the Satan block (top row, third block). In the *Pictorial Quilt*, the eyes seem very curious. In addition to several animals having appliquéd eyes, some animals have ink-drawn eyes. More curiously, three of the figures have ink-drawn eyes. Specifically, the *Pictorial Quilt* blocks with ink-drawn eyes are:

---

[213] "Maxim Karolik Dies; A Patron of the Arts," Newport Daily News, Dec. 21, 1963.

[214] Will of Maxim Karolik, Newport, RI, May 12, 1960.

[215] A note dated May 13, 1964 in the *Pictorial Quilt* file at the Textile Department, Museum of Fine Arts, Boston recommended the acceptance of the quilt as a bequest of Maxim Karolik, through his executor Henry H. Meyer of Rackemann, Sawyer and Brewster in Boston, MA.

Block 3:   Moses with a serpent, women bringing their children for healing. The serpent and the white cloth woman figure have ink-drawn eyes.

Block 4:   Adam and Eve and the Serpent in the Garden of Eden. The small animals, perhaps birds, each have one ink-drawn eye.

Block 5:   A dove descending upon Jesus and John the Baptist after Christ is baptized. The dove has an ink-drawn eye.

Middle Row – left to right

Block 6:   Jonah being thrown over a boat and swallowed by a whale. The two white cloth male figures in the boat and the two turtles have ink-drawn eyes.

Block 7:   The creation of male and female animals. Harriet Powers appliquéd the eyes on three pairs of animals in this block. The other three pairs have ink-drawn eyes.

Block 9:   More pairs of animals. Harriet Powers appliquéd eyes onto three animals. Three other animals have ink-drawn eyes.

Block 10:   Angels are called by God to pour seven vials of wrath. The angel with the white colored trumpet has ink-drawn eyes. The other two angels have no eyes. The one animal in this block has two wide-open ink drawn eyes and cute curly eyelashes. No other animal or figure in either of Powers' known quilts have eyelashes.

Bottom Row – left to right

Block 11:   The results of unusual heavy Georgia snowfall in February 1895. The small white animal at the bottom of this block has one ink-drawn eye.

Block 14:   More pairs of animals. Harriet Powers appliquéd eyes onto five of the animals. The white cloth animals each have ink-drawn eyes. Even the polka dot animal on the left humorously has an ink spot drawn onto one of the polka dots to simulate an eye.

In the *Bible Quilt*, the bedcover owned by the Smithsonian, Harriet Powers seemed to appliqué eyes sparingly. The Devil was the single figure with eyes. Powers only appliquéd eyes onto animals made with solid colored fabrics. She hand-stitched contrasting fabrics to make the eyes, which still seem to pop even now, more than a hundred years after the quilt was created.

In the *Pictorial Quilt,* nearly every animal has eyes, either by appliqué or ink. The appliqué eyes, again, were stitched with contrasting colors and pop off the faces of the animals. By contrast, the ink-drawn eyes are simple outlines. Why would Harriet Powers use these two different creative devices to make eyes on this quilt and not on the *Bible Quilt?*

Was Harriet Powers having fun with viewers of the *Pictorial Quilt* by adding cute, curly eyelashes to the animal in Block 10 or by placing an eye inside of a polka dot on the animal in Block 14?

A Young Artist Adds to the Pictorial Quilt

The *Pictorial Quilt* was first displayed in public in 1975 as part of the "American Bed Furnishing" exhibit at the Museum of Fine Arts, Boston. It would be a number of years until the extended family of Dr. Charles Cuthbert Hall would see the *Pictorial Quilt* again in person.

Robert Utter, a great-grandson of Dr. Charles C. Hall and son of Anne Hall Utter and George Utter, has fond memories of the *Pictorial Quilt*, which he and his younger sister played with as children when it hung in Synton House.[216] He remembered they made up stories for each of the quilt's blocks. He associated the quilt with simple, pleasurable play. Robert was about seven or eight years old when his grandfather, Rev. Basil Hall, sold the *Pictorial Quilt* to Maxim Karolik.

In 2001, several Museum of Fine Arts curators collaborated on "American Folk," an exhibit showcasing the museum's growing collection of folk art in the form of paintings, carvings, prints, furniture, and, of course, textiles. Gerald W. R. Ward, curator of American

---

216 Robert Utter, telephone interview with the author, Mar. 27, 2008.

Decorative Arts and Sculpture at the museum, wrote in the exhibit's catalog that Harriet Powers' *Pictorial Quilt*, a prominent object in the show, was "arguably the single most important example of folk art held by the Museum."[217]

Robert Utter remembered the first time he saw the beloved quilt as an adult. He was about forty-eight years old. The occasion was the much publicized and well-attended "American Folk" exhibition.

"Mother organized a trip to see the quilt at the museum," he shared during an interview at The Other Tiger, the bookstore he owns in Westerly, Rhode Island.[218] "I dreaded seeing the quilt. I sensed that I might have done something to the quilt or dreamt I might have."

"The whole family was there," he said of the trip to the Museum of Fine Arts. "Then I saw it and yes, I realized that I had done something. I was a little shocked, queasy."

As a child, Robert Utter used an ordinary Bic® ballpoint pin with black ink to create eyes on the animals in the *Pictorial Quilt* that had no appliquéd eyes![219]

"I never told anyone," he confessed.

While at the museum, Robert Utter showed his older sister, Katie, where he drew the inked eyes. According to Utter, she immediately turned around and announced aloud in the museum's gallery, "My brother did the eyes!"[220]

"Mother was appalled," he said, "though she later laughed about it."

Robert Utter himself was amused when the Museum of Fine Arts sold pillows featuring blocks from the *Pictorial Quilt*. The ink-drawn eyes were faithfully represented.

"I'm now in reproduction," said Utter.

---

[217] Gerald W. R. Ward and others, American Folk, (Boston: Museum of Fine Arts, 2001), p. 14.

[218] Robert Utter, in-person interview with the author, May 22, 2008.

[219] Utter interview, Mar. 27, 2008.

[220] Utter interview, May 22, 2008.

In Summary

What a chain of custody! Harriet Powers' *Pictorial Quilt* was given as a beloved gift to Dr. Charles C. Hall, a prominent minister who championed the cause of higher education for African Americans. The quilt stayed safely in the Hall family home, Synton House, for decades. Powers' cherished Bible stories, stitched on a farm in Athens, Georgia, hung on a wall in Synton House, just blocks from the cool sea breezes of Westport Harbor, Massachusetts. One generation of Hall great-grandchildren, we now know, holds fond memories of creating make-believe stories based on the quilt's blocks.

For reasons we still can only imagine, in 1960, Rev. Basil Hall drove from Westport Point to Boston to ask whether the Museum of Fine Arts would purchase the *Pictorial Quilt*. Rev. Hall may not even have had a formal appointment when he arrived at the museum. But, Adolph S. Cavallo, the museum's Textile Curator, warmly welcomed the pastor with his cloth bundle anyway.

Within a short period of time, Cavallo encouraged a connection between Rev. Basil Hall and Maxim Karolik, a wealthy widower and famed benefactor of the museum. It is arguable that Martha Codman Karolik, Maxim Karolik's wife, was as wealthy as she was because the inheritance she received from her mother and father - and the successful outcome of a three-year legal battle with her father's mistress over her father's estate.

Maxim Karolik purchased the *Pictorial Quilt* from Rev. Hall for the benefit of the Museum of Fine Arts, where it is kept today.

Who Made The Connection Between The Powers' Quilts?

We take for granted that there are two quilts by Harriet Powers in major museums. The *Bible Quilt* and the *Pictorial Quilt* have never been exhibited together. In fact, it is unclear whether the two quilts were ever in Harriet Powers' home at the same time. How, then, do we know she made both quilts? Who made the connection between the quilts since, there is seemingly no nineteenth-century record that mentions both quilts in the same document?

Again, Aldoph Cavallo provides the answer. In 1971, he was in Washington, D.C. on business. He had an appointment to see Doris Bowman, then Lace and Needlework Specialist at the Division of Textiles of the National Museum of History and Technology. He was early for his meeting.

"I was wandering around the museum before my appointment with Doris Bowman," said Cavallo.[221] "I was near the [Foucault] Pendulum, which always fascinated me. I looked up and saw a quilt and I stopped cold turkey."

The quilt was Harriet Powers' *Bible Quilt*.

The quilt had been on display at the National Museum of History and Technology since April 1969. At the time, the Smithsonian knew only a few details, such as the quiltmakers' first name and hometown.

Cavallo excitedly shared with Bowman that the *Bible Quilt* had many similarities with the *Pictorial Quilt* at the Museum of Fine Arts, Boston: design, composition, construction, fabrics used, themes expressed, and even the quiltmaker's first name and home town.

The *Pictorial Quilt* had not yet been on public display. In fact, it was not until April 1975 that the quilt was included in a major exhibit. Cavallo was one of only a few museum professionals who could have made the connection between the two quilts.

In May 1971, Doris Bowman wrote to the Museum of Fine Arts, Boston and shared the news that Cavallo suggested a connection between the two quilts.[222] She also shared a photograph and described what she knew about the *Bible Quilt*.

Larry Salmon, then Acting Curator of Textiles at the Museum of Fine Arts, wrote back outlining what the Boston museum knew about the *Pictorial Quilt*. He also mailed a photograph of the quilt. Thus, it became clear from our contemporary perspective that Harriet Powers was the quiltmaker of both extraordinary coverings.

---

[221] Aldoph S. Cavallo, telephone interview with the author, Nov. 1, 2008.

[222] The 1971 correspondence between both museums are located in the files of the Textile Department, Museum of Fine Arts, Boston.

Bibliography

Major Works about Harriet Powers and Her Quilts

The following major works are "must have" references to any research about Harriet Powers. These references offer in-depth insights into Powers and her two known, surviving quilts.

Adams, Marie Jeanne. "The Harriet Powers Pictorial Quilts." Black Art: An International Quarterly, vol. 3, no. 4, 1979, pp. 12— 28. Also in William Ferris, ed., Afro-American Folk Art and Crafts (Jackson: University Press of Mississippi, 1983). Also in Judith Weisenfeld and Richard Newman, ed., This Far by Faith: Readings in African-American Women's Religious Biography. (New York: Routledge, 1996). Excellent, in-depth article that takes a critical view of both Powers quilts. Adams writes: "The work of Harriet Powers fits into the category of folk art… Harriet Powers's style of storytelling and composition belong to this folk tradition of image-making. Nevertheless her subject matter draws on the world-church doctrines of Christianity and she has formed the quilt by piecing together milled cloth and applying the figures by sewing machine." Later Adams writes: "The loving spirit in which Mrs. Powers handles the pictorial and decorative elements makes exploration of every part of the quilt a pleasurable and rewarding pursuit." In one of Adams' footnotes, she says the *Pictorial Quilt* was given to Dr. Charles Cuthbert Hall (1852— 1908) "in gratitude for his help in establishing Emory College." She does not provide a citation for the source of the Emory College connection. According to the Emory College website (http://www.college.emory.edu/about), the college was founded in 1836 in Oxford, Georgia. Emory University was later established in 1915 in Atlanta. It is unlikely Dr. Hall helped to establish Emory College given these key dates. The footnote also says Maxim Karolik purchased the *Pictorial Quilt* from the Hall family for $800. This is the first reference in major articles about Harriet Powers to mention a specific price. No specific source for the payment amount, however, is given. [Karolik purchased the *Pictorial Quilt* for $500, according to letters at the Massachusetts Historical Society.]

"Aged Colored Woman Dies in Athens." Athens Banner, January 4, 1910, p. 8. The newspaper reports that "Harriett Powers, an aged negro woman who held the esteem of many Athens people, died from pneumonia Jan 1st. Her remains were carried to her old home near this city for interment Sunday."

"Appliqué Quilt." Bulletin (Museum of Fine Arts, Boston), vol. LXII, no. 330, 1964, pp. 162—163. The recent museum acquisitions are described. This is likely the article from which many of the earliest Powers researchers read that the *Pictorial Quilt* (referred to as the Appliquéd Quilt) was exhibited at the "Nashville Exposition" (quotes in the article), bought by "faculty ladies" and given to the "Chairman of the Board of Trustees of Atlanta University." I have found no evidence, though it may exist, that indicates the *Pictorial Quilt* was ever on display at what is presumably the Tennessee Centennial Exposition, held from May 1 to October 30, 1897. Nor have I located evidence from Atlanta University records to suggest that Dr. Charles Hall was ever the "chairman" of the Board of Trustees, though Dr. Hall was indeed Vice President of the Board.

The earliest known published description of the *Pictorial Quilt* is recorded in this article:

> "Although naïve in subject matter, the effectiveness of the simple shapes which represent animals, birds and figures, and the sensitive placement of these shapes in the bedcover's fifteen rectangular divisions, reflect a highly sophisticated aesthetic sense. An unusual color scheme combining pieces of beige, pink, mauve, orange, dark red, gray-green and several shades of dark blue cotton further testifies to the designer's pleasing and individual taste. To create surface interest, the needlewoman has applied fragments of small scale printed cotton, in conjunction with pieces of solid color, to the large rectangles of monochrome cotton."

The article goes onto say that "[e]nhancing the visual charm of the quilt are the descriptive captions which Mrs. Powers wrote for each of the fifteen scenes." The Museum received, along with the *Pictorial Quilt,* fifteen squares with handwritten descriptions for each of the quilt blocks and a tiny photograph of Harriet Powers all mounted on a board and elegantly framed. There is no text with the descriptions to suggest the writer was indeed Harriet Powers. A second handwritten note, in a different style of handwriting, below the blocks says the quilt was a gift to Dr. Hall and that the quiltmaker was a Negro woman named Harriet Powers.

The photograph in this 1964 article is likely the first-ever published image of the *Pictorial Quilt*, unless a photograph of the quilt was published when it was presented in 1898 to Dr. Charles C. Hall.

Bowman, Doris. Letter to Larry Salmon, MFA Acting Curator of Textiles, May 25, 1971. Department of Textiles and Costumes Files, Museum of Fine Arts, Boston. Bowman shares that Adolph Cavallo recently saw the *Bible Quilt* and suggested the MFA owned a quilt by the same quiltmaker. Bowman requested more information. Enclosures: photograph of the *Bible Quilt* and block descriptions.

Cash, Floris Barnett. "Kinship and Quilting: An Examination of an African-American Tradition." The Journal of Negro History, vol. 80, no. 1, Winter 1995, pp. 30-41, extensive endnotes. Historical survey of African American quilting from slavery time through the Civil Rights and Women's Movements. One page is devoted to Harriet Powers. A distinctive feature of this article is that it provides insights on Dr. Charles C. Hall, who was given the *Pictorial Quilt* in 1898.

"The Colored Race at Atlanta." The Broad Ax (Salt Lake City, UT), December 7, 1895, pp. 1, 4. This extensive article is four columns long. While not naming Harriet Powers specifically, the reporter's eyewitness account of the fair demonstrates how spectacular the *Bible Quilt* must have been. Several quilts were displayed in the Negro Building of the Fair. The *Bible Quilt* was displayed in a "corner reserved for the work of the ex-slaves of this country." While there is no reporter byline listed, it is likely this article was written by Clara R. Jemison.

Lorene Curtis Diver File, 1 Folder. Raymond E. Garrison Files. Lee County Historical Society, Miller House Museum, 318 N. 5th Street, Keokuk, IA 52632. Phone (319) 524-7283. Included:

- "Sermon in Patchwork" photograph of the *Bible Quilt*, 1895-96. Handwritten descriptions in Diver's hand. Bright exposure. Likely a professional photograph. Photographer unknown.
- "Sermon in Patchwork" photograph of the *Bible Quilt*, 1895-96. Darker exposure. Photographer unknown, though likely Diver.
- *Carte de visite* of Powers by McDannell Studios, ca. 1896-97.

- Copy of letter from Harriet Powers and Jennie Smith, 2 pages. The copy appears to be in Lorene Diver's handwriting.
- Typed draft of the letters dated 1969.
- "A Sermon in Patchwork" article by Lorene Finch, *Outlook*, October 26, 1914. Appears to be an original copy.
- Family photograph of Lorene Diver as a child with her parents and siblings. Taped on the photo is a tiny snapshot of an elderly woman, presumably an adult Lorene Diver.

Faubion, Trish. "To Tell a Story: Harriet Powers and the Religious – Narrative Traditions in African American Quilts." Piecework, May/June 1994, pp. 40—47. Well-worth reading. Comprehensive article that summarizes the research to 1994 on Harriet Powers by John Vlach ("special creations in which the memory of Africa is sometimes quite strong"), Cuesta Benberry (Powers' motifs might have been influenced by Black fraternal orders or benevolent societies), and Maude Wahlman (Powers' motifs work on four levels: African, Christian, Masonic, and "allude to the Underground Railroad."). Faubion also mentions contemporary African American quilters who have created Bible-themed quilts such as Viola Canady, Peggie Hartwell, Anita Holman Knox, Lorraine Mahan, and Yvonne Wells. The two-page photo spread of the *Pictorial Quilt* is in reverse.

Finch, Lucine. "A Sermon in Patchwork." Outlook, a weekly journal edited by Rev. Dr. Lyman Abbott, vol. 108, October 26, 1914. The illustrated patchwork quilt, though not identified by name, is Harriet Powers' *Bible Quilt*. The 1914 article includes a photograph of the quilt. It is unclear who took the photograph. Mrs. Powers is referred to as the "aged Negro woman." The article explains the meaning behind each quilt block. Finch writes, "It is the reverent, worshipful embodiment of an old colored woman's soul. I shall use her own words, in as far as I can quote them." It is unclear when or whether Finch spoke directly to Harriet Powers, who died in 1910, as it is not recorded in the article. Reprinted in Singular Women: Writing the Artist, eds. Kristen Frederickson and Sarah E. Webb, Berkeley: University of California Press, 2003, pp. 95—99.

Freeman, Roland. A Communion of the Spirits: African-American Quilters, Preservers, and Their Stories. Nashville, TN: Rutledge Hill Press, 1996. Information on Harriet Powers is on pages 101—104. Freeman outlines the 1992 controversy when the Smithsonian

Institution decided to reproduce several historical quilts in its collection, including the *Bible Quilt*. On page 103 is a photograph Freeman took of five descendants of Harriet Powers posing in front of Powers' quilt at the Boston Museum of Fine Arts. This was the first time this branch of the family saw the quilt in person.

Fry, Gladys-Marie. "Harriet Powers: Portrait of a Black Quilter." In Missing Pieces: Georgia Folk Art 1770—1976, edited by Anna Wadsworth. Atlanta: Georgia Council for the Arts and Humanities, 1976, pp. 16—23. Also found in Sage: A Scholarly Journal on Black Women vol. 4, no. 1, Spring 1987, pp. 11—16. Fry explains that Powers incorporated three types of oral traditional stories in her quilts: 1) local legends, 2) biblical stories, and 3) accounts of astronomical events. Fry compares Powers' appliqué interpretations to Dahomean tapestries. Fry also shares U.S. Census and county tax record details about the Powers family. Fry suggests that "[a]pparently Armsted left the family and the farm" some time after 1894 based on Armsted's name not appearing on subsequent tax rolls with his wife's name. Fry suggests that "[f]rom 1894 to 1910 Harriet maintained herself quite independently."

Fry, Gladys-Marie. "A Sermon in Patchwork: New Light on Harriet Powers." In Singular Women: Writing the Artist, edited by Kristen Frederickson and Sarah E. Webb. Berkeley: University of California Press, 2003, pp. 81—94. Dr. Fry shares her personal reflections since starting to research Harriet Powers' life in the early 1970s. Sections of the essay include: The Jenny Smith Connection, A Brief Overview of Harriet Powers's Life and Her Artistic Inspiration, Lucine Finch: A Second Eyewitness, Harriet Powers Discusses Her Quilt, and A Spiritual Connection.

Fry, Gladys-Marie. Stitched From the Soul: Slave Quilts from the Ante-Bellum South. Foreword by Dr. Robert Bishop. New York: Dutton Studio Books, 1990. Subjects covered in this book include the slave seamstress, quilting in the slave quarters, and differences in types of quilting parties. The comprehensive profile of Harriet Powers found in Missing Pieces is reprinted here as the Epilogue.

Holmes, Catherine L. "The Darling Offspring of Her Brain." In Georgia Quilts: Piecing Together a History, edited by Anita Zaleski Weinraub. Athens: University of Georgia Press, 2006, pp. 174–187, notes 270—271. An exciting article with newly discovered, well-cited facts about Harriet Powers. Holmes is the researcher who rediscovered Harriet Powers' gravesite and located a newspaper obituary that indicated she passed away in 1910, not 1911 as widely published.

Jemison, Clara R. "Exhibit of the Negroes: Monument to Their Material Progress Seen in Atlanta: Some of the Wonders of the Colored People's Contributions at the Cotton States Exhibition." <u>Chicago Daily</u>, November 24, 1895, p. 30. Extensive article about several Negro Building exhibits, including Powers' *Bible Quilt.*

Lyons, Mary E. <u>Stitching Stars: The Story Quilts of Harriet Powers</u>. New York: Charles Scribner's Sons, 1993. 42 p. This story for young readers is about Harriet Powers in the context of American nineteenth-century American life. Engaging story and color photographs holds a child's attention, but no footnotes for adults. Lyons writes that Powers was the mother of eleven children on page 1, though no citations are given to substantiate this claim. On page 36, Lyons writes that "[b]y 1900 only three of her children were still alive." Lyons notes that Powers "cut out 299 separate pieces of cloth" to make her *Bible Quilt.*

Collection of Harriet Powers books in the author's personal library.

Museum of Fine Arts, Boston. <u>A Pattern Book, Based on Appliqué Quilt by Mrs. Harriet Powers, American, 19<u>th</u> Century</u>. Boston: Museum of Fine Arts, 1973. [32] p. This paperback book describes each of the fifteen blocks. There is one pattern per page. Each pattern is reduced 58% from its original size. The book is about 9.5 in. x 12 in. No editor or artist for the blocks is listed.

Betty Riegel, who ran the Museum of Fine Arts, Boston gift shop, asked the museum's publications department to create a book featuring the *Pictorial Quilt* pattern, according to Carl Zahn, retired MFA Publications Director. "She thought it would sell well," he said in a September 11, 2008 phone interview with Kyra Hicks. Sue Chapman, from the museum's Egyptian department, created the drawings for each block. Zahn designed the book.

Perry, Regenia A. "Harriet Powers (1837—1910)." In <u>Selections of Nineteenth-Century Afro-American Art</u> (exhibition catalog). New York: Metropolitan Museum of Art, 1976. [42] p. The exhibit lasted from June 19 to August 1, 1976 in honor of America's Bicentennial celebration. There is one full page description of the *Pictorial Quilt* (page 3) and one page devoted to a photograph of the quilt.

Perry, Regenia A. <u>Harriet Powers's Bible Quilts</u>. New York: Rizzoli International Publications, Inc. Large-format book, 14 in. x 10 in., 1994. [24] p. Overview of Harriet Powers's life. Detailed photos and descriptions are presented for both quilts by Powers.

Powers, Harriet A. Copy of letter to Lorene Diver, January 1896. Lorene Curtis Diver File, Lee County Historical Society, Keokuk, IA.

Salmon, Larry. Duplicate copy of letter to Doris M. Bowman, Lace and Needlework Specialist, Division of Textiles, Smithsonian Institution, National Museum of History and Technology, June 29, 1971. Department of Textiles and Costumes files, Museum of Fine Arts, Boston. Salmon agrees with Adolph Cavallo's suggestion that the *Bible Quilt* and the *Pictorial Quilt* are both likely created by Harriet Powers. Salmon provides biographical information about Powers, *Pictorial Quilt* photograph, and block descriptions.

Shearer, Lee. "Famous Grave Found Off Fourth Street." <u>Athens Banner-Herald</u>, January 10, 2005. Detailed account of the rediscovery of Harriet and Armsted Powers' final resting place in the Gospel Pilgrim Cemetery in Athens, Georgia by University of Georgia graduate student, Cat Holmes. The article mentions that both Harriet and her husband's names are on the headstone, which measured "about 15 inches by about two feet and about ¾ of an inch thick." The article also mentions that Holmes located the headstone for "Viola Powers, one of Harriet's daughters."

Shearer, Lee. "History Rediscovered in Athens." Florida Times Union (Jacksonville, FL–Georgia edition), January 11, 2005. Detailed account of Athens native and former newspaper editor Cat Holmes' successful two-year effort to locate the grave site of Harriet Powers at the Gospel Pilgrim Cemetery. According to the article, the eleven-acre cemetery was founded in 1882 as an African American burial ground. The remains of approximately 3,000 persons rest there.

Smith, Jennie. "A Biblical Quilt." Handwritten essay, not dated. Textile Department, Smithsonian Museum of American History, Washington, D.C. Smith writes from her home at 129 Washington Street, Athens, Georgia about the 1886 "Cotton Fair," which included a Wild West show and a circus. At this Fair, Smith first sees the *Bible Quilt*. Smith records Powers' first name as "Harriett." She writes Powers is "about sixty-five years old, of a burnt ginger cake color, and is a very clean and interesting woman who loves to talk of her "ole Miss." Smith also describes how she came to purchase the quilt and her intentions to exhibit the quilt at the upcoming Cotton States Exposition in Atlanta in the segregated Colored Building. Finally, Smith describes each of the quilt's eleven blocks based on Powers' narrative about the pieces. This nine-page essay has a tiny hole at the top of each page, as if the pages were once tacked onto a corked bulletin board. It is kept in a small mint-green colored envelope. Harold Heckman, Smith's executor, donated both this document and the *Bible Quilt* to the Smithsonian in 1969.

Smith, Jennie. Copy of Letter to Lorene Diver, September 1894 (Based on the content of the letter, the correct date is likely 1895). Lorene Curtis Diver File, Lee County Historical Society, Keokuk, IA.

United States Census. The following is a partial list of U.S. Census data related to Harriet Powers and her family.

1870, Clarke County, Sandy Creek, Georgia: Armsted Powers (age 38, Farm hand, value of personal estate $300), Harriet (34, Keeping house), Amanda (15, at house), Leonzoe (10), and Nancy (4). Armsted, Harriet, and Amanda are listed as not able to read or write. Leonzoe is likely misspelled and should be Alonzo.

1880, Clarke County, Sandy Creek, Georgia: Armsted Powell (age 48, married, laborer, can not read or write), Harriet (42, wife, married, keeping house), Alonzo C. (19, son, single, laborer), Lizzie (12, daughter, laborer, can not write), Marshall (7, son). The family name is misspelled as Powell, not Powers. This census indicates Harriet and her son, Alonzo, *can*, indeed, read and write.

1900, Clarke County, Sandy Creek, Georgia: Armsted Powers (age 67, Head, born September 1832, farmer, owned own home with a mortgage), Harriet (62, wife, born October 1837, nine children born to her and three living). The records indicate the couple was married forty-four years, both were born in Georgia, and neither could read or write.

1900, Clarke County, Buck Branch, Georgia: Alonzo Powers (age 35, head, born May 1865, married twenty years, rents their house, minister), Julia (35, wife, born February 1865, married 20 years, twelve children, six living), Alonzo R. (15, son, farm laborer, born February 1885), Nann C. (13, son, farm laborer, born August 1886), Lizzie A. (12, daughter, at school, born October 1887), Julia O. (5, daughter, born May 1895), Netty (2, daughter, born December 1897), and Susan (3 months, daughter, born February 1900). The census indicates Alonzo, Julia, Alonzo R., and Nann can read and write.

Vlach, John Michael. The Afro-American Traditions in Decorative Art. Cleveland, OH: Cleveland Museum of Art, 1978. *Quilting* chapter is on pages 44—75. The chapter includes a discussion about Harriet Powers, photos of her two known quilts, and detailed quilt descriptions. The essay argues that Powers' appliqué technique is "generally similar to methods known both in Europe and Africa." On page 48, he states, "The presence of West African slaves in Georgia makes it possible, then, to link Mrs. Powers' quilts to African aesthetic systems." He goes on to show pictures of works by the Fon of Benin that closely resemble the Powers' style.

Books and Exhibit Catalogs

Abdullah, Omanii. I Wanna Be the Kinda Father My Mother Was. New York: Signal Hill, 1993. Book of lovely, meaningful poems. The first poem in this 64-page volume bears the title of the book and showcases Harriet Powers' *Pictorial Quilt*.

Bacon, Lenice Ingram. American Patchwork Quilt. New York: William Morrow, 1973. See pages 95–96 for the Harriet Powers quilt in Museum of Fine Arts, Boston.

Bank, Mirra. Anonymous Was a Woman: A Celebration in Words and Images of Traditional American Art and the Women Who Made It. New York: St. Martin's Griffin, 1995. See pages 118–119 for details and photo of the *Pictorial Quilt*.

Benberry, Cuesta. Always There: The African-American Presence in American Quilts. Louisville, KY: The Kentucky Quilt Project, Inc., 1992. See pages 43–47 for the chapter titled "Bible Quilts." Benberry examines various quilts made by Black women using the Bible as inspiration.

Benjamin, Tritobia Hayes. "Triumphant Determination: The Legacy of African American Women Artists." In Bearing Witness: Contemporary Works by African American Women Artists. Curated by Jontyle Theresa Robinson. New York: Spelman College and Rizzoli International Publications, 1996. See pp. 49–81. Benjamin places Harriet Powers in the context of other Black women artists – both folk and fine artists. Photo of the *Pictorial Quilt* is included. Jontyle Theresa Robinson compiled an excellent chronology of Black women artists from 1619–1996.

Berlo, Janet Catherine. "Chronicles in Cloth: Quilt-making and Female Artistry in Nineteenth-Century America. In Local/Global: Women Artists in the Nineteenth Century, edited by Deborah Cherry and Janice Helland. Aldershot (England): Ashgate, 2006. See pp. 201—222. This essay includes a discussion about Harriet Powers. Specifically, Dr. Berlo argues that Powers' work should be examined from her local American, American quilt history, and American appliqué technique context, not reaching back to West Africa textile practices. She argues, "I would assert...Harriet Powers...and countless other women before her, is a quintessential American artist, working in a genre popular among both black and white quilters alike in the nineteenth century, and using her talent and ingenuity to express a keen interest in Bible stories and wondrous events from oral history.... Divorcing her important works of art from their local context does an injustice to Harriet Powers..."

Blount, Brian K., Cain Hope Felder, Clarice Jannette Martin, and Emerson B. Powery. True to Our Native Land: An African American New Testament Commentary. Minneapolis: Fortress Press, 2007. The Powers quilts are featured on pages 47 and 53.

Boisvert, Donald J. 500 Tomato Plants in the Kitchen: 50 Stories, Articles and Essays with a Rhode Island-New England Flavor. Xlibris Corporation, 2001. The essay, "Florence Nightingale's Cap," on pages 49—61, provides the history of how a lace head cover owned by famed British nurse Florence Nightingale ended up on display at the Westerly, Rhode Island Hospital. The cap was a gift from Mrs. Anna Loraine Washburn Hall, the great-granddaughter of Cyrus Hamlin, to whom Nightingale gave the cap. Mrs. Hall was the wife of Rev. Basil Douglass Hall. The *Pictorial Quilt* by Harriet Powers was once in the family of Rev. and Mrs. Hall.

Bowman, Doris M. The Smithsonian Treasury American Quilts– National Museum of American History. Washington, DC: Smithsonian Institution Press, 1991. African American quilts in the Smithsonian's collection are: *Frances Jolly's Quilt*, a quilt top; *Ann's Quilt*, a slave-made quilt; *Betty West's Quilt*; and Harriet Powers' *Bible Quilt*, with detailed explanations for each of the quilt blocks. See pp. 80 – 81, 95.

Cavalieri, Grace. Quilting the Sun. Bloomington, IL: GOSS183 Casa Menendez, 2009. Publication of the play *Quilting the Sun*, a fictional account of why Harriet Powers sold her *Bible Quilt* to Jennie Smith.

Cavallo, Adolph S. Needlework. New York: Cooper-Hewitt Museum, 1979. Cavallo provides insights into needlework techniques and examples from the West, East, Western Asia, the Near East as well as from indigenous peoples of Africa and America. Powers' *Bible Quilt* is featured on page 76. Cavallo was the Textile Curator at the Museum of Fine Arts, Boston when it acquired the *Pictorial Quilt*.

Chicago, Judy, and Susan Hill. Embroidering Our Heritage: The Dinner Party Needlework. Garden City, NY: Anchor Books, 1980. The *Pictorial Quilt* is featured on page 222.

Cliff, Michelle. "I Found God in Myself and I Loved Her/I Loved Her Fiercely": More Thoughts on the Work of Black Women Artists. In Women, Feminist Identity, and Society in the 1980's: Selected Papers. Critical Theory, v.1 edited by Myriam Díaz-Diocaretz and Iris M. Zavala. Amsterdam: Benjamins, 1985. Cliff's essay is on pages101—126. Michelle Cliff says of Powers on page 111:

> "It is my opinion that we should approach the quilts of Harriet Powers as the work of an artist both conscious of and in control of her images, and that the view needs to recognize that there is a plan to the construction of the work of art, in which the frames can be seen in relation to each other as well as separate scenes which convey messages."

Dallas Museum of Art. Black Art Ancestral Legacy: The African Impulse in African-American Art. Dallas, TX: Dallas Museum of Art, 1989. See pp. 38—39.

Dewhurst, C. Kurt, et. al. Artists in Aprons: Folk Art by American Women. New York: E.P. Dutton in association with the Museum of American Folk Art, 1979. Includes references to Clementine Hunter, Harriet Powers and other Black female folk artists on pages 49, 54 – 55, 82, 94, and 169.

Dewhurst, C. Kurt, Betty MacDowell, and Marsha MacDowell. Religious Folk Art in America: Reflections of Faith. New York: E.P. Dutton in association with the Museum of American Folk Art, 1983. Harriet Powers is referenced on pages 47 and 92. Photo of the *Pictorial Quilt* included. The photo captions said that "[r]ecently, another quilt similar to hers has surfaced in Tennessee," though no citation or other insights are provided. Given we now know Powers stitched at least five quilts, it is important to follow-up on this lead!

Farrington, Lisa E. Creating Their Own Image: The History of African-American Women Artists. Oxford: Oxford University Press, 2005. See pp. 38 – 41. Farrington's text suggests that Harriet Powers "had knowledge of the Underground Railroad code and that she may have been a member of a Masonic order that participated in Underground Railroad activity." The sources Farrington uses for these suggestions are *Hidden in Plain View* and *Signs and Symbols*. Farrington later suggests that "Powers's treatment of ambiguous ground planes, streamlined forms, and certain figural motifs prefigure the "jazz" cutouts of French modernist Henri Matisse."

Ferrero, Pat, Elaine Hedges and Julie Silber. Hearts and Hands: The Influence of Women and Quilts in American Society. San Francisco: Quilt Digest Press, 1987. Text and photograph of the *Pictorial Quilt* are on pages 45–48. The authors write poignantly about Powers' two quilts: "These two known nineteenth-century examples, by their very existence, sophistication and wholeness, can only begin to suggest what has been lost."

Ferris, William R. Afro-American Folk Art and Crafts. Center for the Study of Southern Culture series. Jackson: University Press of Mississippi, 1986. Harriet Powers is mentioned in the section on Quilt Makers, starting on page 65.

Fox, Sandi. Wrapped in Glory: Figurative Quilts & Bedcovers, 1700-1900. New York: Thames and Hudson, 1990. Thirty-six rare quilts are included in the first exhibition in this area by the Los Angeles County Museum of Art. Both of Harriet Powers' quilts are featured in the book on pages 136–141, though neither was on actual display in Los Angeles. Surprisingly, the text states: "Technically, both quilts are crudely constructed, but on the strength of their astounding aesthetic and narrative qualities, they stand as two of America's greatest figurative quilts."

Georges, Robert A., and Michael Owens Jones. Folkloristics: An Introduction. Bloomington: Indiana University Press, 1995. Chapter nine focuses on folklore as a personal resource. This textbook examines Harriet Powers in the context of reviewing the role of folklore in the life of one deceased. See pages 270–274.

Grudin, Eva Ungar. Stitching Memories: African-American Story Quilts. Williamstown, MA: Williams College Museum of Art, 1990. Text about Harriet Powers is on page 16. Image of the *Pictorial Quilt* is on page 6.

Hall, Basil Douglas. The Life of Charles Cuthbert Hall: "One Among a Thousand". New York: Carlton Press, 1965. The *Pictorial Quilt* by Harriet Powers was given as a gift to Charles C. Hall. This book is written by his eldest son and includes twenty chapters and a two-page chronology. There is no mention of the quilt in this book. Mrs. Katherine Hall Preston, one of Basil Hall's daughters, privately published an extended version of this book, which included the original text prior to editing, in 1997.

Hausman, Gerald, and Kelvin Rodriques. African-American Alphabet: A Celebration of African-American and West Indian Culture, Custom, Myth, and Symbol. New York: St. Martin's Press, 1996. See *Q—Quilt* on pp. 141—144. Includes poem by Terri Lynne Singleton "We Call Your Name, Harriet Powers."

Hedges, Elaine, and Ingrid Wendt, eds. In Her Own Image: Women Working in the Arts. New York: The Feminist Press, 1980. Includes feature about Harriet Powers.

Hester, Al. Gospel Pilgrim Cemetery: An African-American Historic Site. Athens, GA: Green Berry Press, 2004. Harriet Powers and her husband are buried in this cemetery.

Hester, Albert L. Athens Memories: The WPA Federal Writers' Project Interviews. Athens, GA: Green Berry Press, 2001. Hester rediscovers a Federal Writers' Project, part of the Works Progress administration (WPA), interview with Rev. Alonzo C. Powers, one of Harriet Powers' sons. See the online article by Hester, "Slavery, and What Happened When the Yankees Came Also" at www.freerepublic.com/focus/news/696206/posts (accessed May 25, 2008). In the Appendix, there is additional information on Rev. Powers on pages 223–235. Hester uses census data and other information to confirm elements of Powers' first-person story. Fascinating essay. Must read appendix!

Hicks, Kyra E. Black Threads: An African American Quilting Sourcebook. Jefferson, NC: McFarland & Co, 2003. Includes various bibliographic references to Harriet Powers.

Hine, Darlene Clark, Elsa Barkley Brown, and Rosalyn Terborg-Penn. Black Women in America: An Historical Encyclopedia. Brooklyn, NY: Carlson Publishing, 1993. Kathleen Thompson contributes a bibliographical essay on Harriet Powers on pages 937–938.

hooks, bell. Yearning: Race, Gender, and Cultural Politics. Boston, MA: South End Press, 1990. bell hooks examines the role quilt making plays in the lives of Black women. See the chapter titled "Aesthetic Inheritances: History Worked by Hands" on pages 115–122; Harriet Powers is discussed on page 118.

Kampen-O'Riley, Michael. Art Beyond the West: The Arts of Africa, West and Central Asia, India and Southeast Asia, China, Japan and Korea, the Pacific, Africa, and the Americas. Upper Saddle River,

NJ: Pearson Prentice Hall, 2006. The *Pictorial Quilt* is featured on pages 265–266 in the second edition of this text.

Kirkham, Pat, ed. Women Designers in the USA, 1900 – 2000 Diversity and Difference. New Haven: Yale University Press, 2000. Chapters include "Three Strikes Against Me: African American Women Designers" and "Tradition and Transformation: Women Quilt Designers." Black quilters mentioned include Ruth Clement Bond, Carol Harris, Carolyn Mazloomi, Harriet Powers (p. 131), Faith Ringgold, Jessie Telfair, Anna Williams, and Lucile Young.

Lewis, Richard, and Susan I. Lewis. The Power of Art. Fort Worth, TX: Harcourt Brace College Publishers, 1995. Mentions the *Pictorial Quilt*.

Lipman, Jean. Five Star Folk Art: One Hundred American Masterpieces. New York: H. N. Abrams in association with the Museum of American Folk Art, 1990. Includes the *Pictorial Quilt.*

Marler, Ruth. The Art of the Quilt. Philadelphia: Courage Books, 2001. Harriet Powers is mentioned on pages 23–24.

Marzio, Peter, ed. A Nation of Nations: The People Who Came to America as Seen Through Objects, Prints, and Photographs at the Smithsonian Institution. New York: Harper & Row, 1976. A full-page image of Powers' *Bible Quilt* and a detailed image of the Devil block are on pages 250–251.

Mason, Rhonda. Daughters of Harriet Powers: Tribute to an American Quilt Maker. Tampa, FL: Museum of African American Art, February 7, 1997 to March 22, 1997. [24] p. This exhibit featured forty-one quilts by twenty-five contemporary quilters.

The show was curated by Rhonda Mason, who was also known by family and friends as Patricia Singleton Sabia. Quilters included Corrine Appleton, Ana N. Arzu, Grace C. Bachman, Alice M. Beasley, Sally Broadwell, C. K. Brown, Rita Denenberg, Judith Geiger, Kianga Hanif, Radiah Harper, Virginia R. Harris, Peggy Hartwell, Leslie Hatch-Wong, Kyra Hicks, Joanna Kilroy, Mary Mashuta, Rhonda Mason, Ed Johnetta Miller, Jane Hardy Miller, Pauline Salzman, Penny Sisto, Barbara A. Stewart, Katharine Stubbs-Ward, Sherry Whetstone-McCall, and Deborah Willis. Exhibition catalog and checklist.

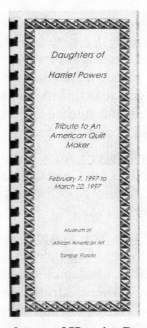

Daughters of
Harriet Powers

Tribute to An
American Quilt
Maker

February 7, 1997 to
March 22, 1997

Museum of
African American Art
Tampa, Florida

Daughters of Harriet Powers
Twenty-four page exhibit catalog and checklist

Curator Rhonda Mason (1948–1997) wrote in the catalog introduction:

> "Powers was, like women of today, a busy mother who worked hard and took excellent care of her family as well. Yet we must look hard – a little too hard to find Harriet Powers in our textbooks. We must look a bit too hard to understand the importance of quilts in the lives of the people who developed and built America. Every household had at least one quilt that was used to keep people warm at night, but do we talk about that? No.

> "This is why I decided to do a show about Harriet Powers – the mother of the American Story Quilt. This show is dedicated to Harriet Powers, her work and her craft from her "daughters" who happen to be some of the finest quilt makers in the United States today."

Two of the quilts in the exhibit directly honored Powers: Joanna Kilroy's *Harriet Powers' Nativity Scene* (no date) and Peggy Hartwell's *Ode To Harriet Powers* (1994).

Massey, Brandon. "Granddad's Garage." In Dark Dreams: A Collection of Horror and Suspense by Black Writers, edited by Brandon Massey, New York: Kensington Publishing, 2004, pp. 219–231. After his granddad's death, a grandson clears out his grandfather's seemingly cluttered garage to find incalculable treasurers, including an 1897 Bible-themed quilt stitched by Harriet Powers. Wonderful, thought-provoking short story!

Mattera, Joanne. The Quiltmaker's Art: Contemporary Quilts and Their Makers. Asheville, NC: Lark Communications, 1982. This book is dedicated to Harriet Powers. No African American quilters seem to be profiled in this book.

Mazloomi, Carolyn. Quilting African American Women's History: Our Challenges, Creativity, and Champions. West Chester, OH: Paper Moon Publishing, 2008. Mazloomi's opening essay is titled "The Daughters of Harriet Powers: African American Women Quilt a Culture" on pages 4–10. Exhibit catalog featuring more than 100 quilts by fifty-six quilters.

Morton, Robert. Southern Antiques and Folk Art. Birmingham, AL: Oxmoor House, 1977. Includes one of Harriet Powers' quilts.

Moyers, Bill D. Genesis: A Living Conversation. New York: Doubleday, 1997. Detail of Adam and Eve block from the Pictorial Quilt is on page 90.

Museum of Fine Arts, Boston, and Gilian Shallcross Wohlauer. MFA: A Guide to the Collection of the Museum of Fine Arts, Boston. Introduction by Malcolm Rogers. Boston: Museum of Fine Arts, 1999. Profile of the Karoliks is located on pages 322–323. Photos of the Pictorial Quilt and two detailed blocks are on page 351.

Museum of Fine Arts, Boston, and Pamela A. Parmal. Textile & Fashion Arts. Boston: MFA Publications, 2006.

Museum of Fine Arts, Boston, and Gerald W. R. Ward. American Folk: Folk Art from the Collection of the Museum of Fine Arts, Boston. Boston: MFA Publications, 2001. The Pictorial Quilt is featured on pages 92–93. The text mistakenly says Harriet Powers died in 1911 and that the quilt was given "as a gift to a retiring trustee." In fact, Powers died in 1910 and Dr. Charles C. Hall was an Atlanta University trustee until his death in 1908.

Painter, Nell Irvin. Creating Black Americans: African-American History and Its Meanings, 1619 to the Present. New York: Oxford University Press, 2006. The *Pictorial Quilt* is on page 51.

Patton, Sharon F. African-American Art. New York: Oxford University Press, 1998. Quilt discussion is on pages 67–71, with particular attention to Harriet Powers.

Perry Regenia A. "Black American Folk Art: Origins and Early Manifestations." In Black Folk Art in America 1930 – 1980, by Jane Livingston and John Beardsley. Jackson: University Press of Mississippi, 1982. Essay includes references to Harriet Powers and her two known quilts in a section on quiltmaking.

Perry, Regenia A. "Powers, Harriet: American Quiltmaker." In St. James Guide to Black Artists, edited by Thomas Riggs. Detroit: St. James Press, 1997. Bibliographical, career information, and brief critical essays on nearly four hundred prominent Black artists. Fiber artists or quilters include Gloretta Baynes, Roland Freeman, Michael D. Harris, Clementine Hunter, Martha Jackson-Jarvis, Napoleon Jones-Henderson, Harriet Powers, Faith Ringgold, and Joyce Scott. The article on Harriet Powers by Regenia A. Perry (page 435) compares and contrasts the two known Powers quilts. The article incorrectly states Powers passed away in 1911.

Pongracz, Patricia, and Carolyn Mazloomi. *Threads of Faith: Recent Works from the Women of Color Quilters Network*. New York: Gallery of the American Bible Society, 2004. Both Powers quilts are included on pages 29–31.

Powell, Richard J. Black Art and Culture in the 20th Century. World of Art. New York: Thames & Hudson, 1997. Harriet Powers and the *Pictorial Quilt* are featured on pages 26 and 28.

Powell, Richard J. "Conjuring Canes and Bible Quilts: Through the Prism of Nineteenth-Century African American Spirituality" in African Americans and the Bible: Sacred Texts and Social Textures by Vincent L. Wimbush and Rosamond C. Rodman. New York: Continuum, 2001. See pages 342–352 for image of the *Bible Quilt*.

Regan, Jennifer. American Quilts: A Sampler of Quilts and Their Stories. New York City: Gallery Books, 1989. Powers' *Pictorial Quilt*, listed here as *Creation of the Animals Quilt*, is featured on page 144 and 147 in the "Personal Visions" chapter.

Rivo, Lisa E. "Powers, Harriet." In The African American National Biography, ed. Henry Louis Gates and Evelyn Brooks Higginbotham. New York: Oxford University Press, 2008. The Biography is an eight-volume set that includes a profile of Harriet Powers. Other Black quilters included are Michael Cummings, Carolyn Mazloomi, and Martha Ann Ricks. The late quilt historian Cuesta Benberry is also included. The Powers biography is on pages 419–421. Rivo cites Fry, Lyons, and Perry. The profile mistakenly states Powers died in 1911. It also gives the incorrect name for the Smithsonian museum that owns the Bible Quilt.

Rydell, Robert W. All the World's a Fair. Chicago: The University of Chicago Press, 1984. Chapter 3, "The New Orleans, Atlanta, and Nashville Expositions: New Markets, "New Negroes," and a New South" is an important resource for learning more about these three events. The Bible Quilt was exhibited at the Atlanta fair.

Safford, Carleton, and Robert Bishop. America's Quilts and Coverlets. New York: Dutton, 1972. A comprehensive guide with emphasis on patchwork and appliqué quilts. Harriet Powers is listed on page 211.

Salmon, Larry, Catherine Kvaraceus, and Matthew X. Kiernan. From Fiber to Fine Art: Handbook of the Department of Textiles. Boston: Museum of Fine Arts, 1980. Includes Harriet Powers' Pictorial Quilt. The exhibit was open from July to September 1980. The introductory essay by Salmon provides an overview of the key individuals responsible for the Textile Department at the Museum of Fine Arts. The acquisition achievements of Adolph S. Cavallo, who was appointed Curator in 1960, are also listed. Cavallo was Curator when the museum acquired Harriet Powers' Pictorial Quilt.

Smith, Cheryl A. Market Women: Black Women Entrepreneurs—Past, Present, and Future. Westport, CT: Praeger Publishers, 2005. A section on quilting entrepreneurs is on pages 60–62. Harriet Powers is mentioned.

Spalding, Phinizy, and Phyllis Jenkins Barrow. Higher Education for Women in the South: A History of Lucy Cobb Institute, 1858-1994. Athens, GA: Georgia Southern Press, 1994. Extensive history of both the school, which closed in 1931, and of efforts to restore historical buildings on the school's campus. Jennie Smith, who purchased the Bible Quilt from Harriet Powers, was a former student of the Lucy Cobb Institute and art teacher from 1880 to 1930. Smith lived on the campus in an old house formerly used by the school's cook and renovated to include living quarters and an art studio for Smith. There was an agreement that Smith could live in the home all her life (pages 44–45), even after the school closed. One essay in the book, "Miss Jennie Smith and Lucy Cobb" by Bessie Mell Lane (pages 273–275), described Smith as a "small and plump" woman who "always wore black, bombazine for dress and fine cotton otherwise – the shirtwaists and flaring skirts of the late nineteenth century which she never gave up. At her neck she always wore a small Irish lace over-collar with a broach at her chin. Her hair was white…and slightly curly but pulled up in a careless knot on the top of her head with wispy strands escaping."

Tate, Susan Frances Barrow. Remembering Athens. Athens, GA: Athens Historical Society, 1996. In the chapter titled, "I Went to Lucy Cobb," are memories of several school teachers, including Jennie Smith. There is one rare photograph on page 58 of Jennie Smith, likely in her 20s or 30s, sitting outside with her friends, Anne Brumby and Susie Gerdine, at a Lucy Cobb Institute event.

Thomas, Frances Taliaferro. A Portrait of Historical Athens and Clarke County. Athens, GA: University of Georgia Press, 1992. Includes information about Jennie Smith and Powers on pages 151–152.

Thomson, Peggy and Edwards Park. The Pilot & the Lion Cub: Odd Tales from the Smithsonian. Washington, D.C.: Smithsonian Institution Press, 1986. Cute tiny book! "How the Bible Became a Quilt" tale is on pages 140–141.

Thurmond, Michael L. Edited by Conoly Hester. A Story Untold: Black Men and Women in Athens History. Edited by Conoly Hester. Athens, GA: Green Berry Press, 1978. Powers is listed among the prominent people and organizations from Athens, Georgia.

Tobin, Jacqueline, and Raymond G. Dobard. Hidden in Plain View: The Secret Story of Quilts and the Underground Railroad. New York: Doubleday, 1999. Tobin and Dobard ask many questions of Harriet Powers and her two quilts. On page 29, the authors "wonder if Powers was a member of an Eastern Star women's association." Later the authors suggest there is secrecy within Powers' quilts and that "[e]xactly all that Powers is stating remains a mystery, a part of her secret world." The authors question "[c]ould not Powers's quilt also be a coded star map, in which she was mapping the heavens as well…?" The authors (on page 124) do not specifically state which of Powers' quilts they are referring to when they question whether one of her quilts could be "coded." Further, the authors ask "[w]as Powers also documenting the Underground Railroad as she had been told about it?" The authors do not provide any first-person documentation or other citation confirming as fact that Harriet Powers knew about the Underground Railroad. On page 125, the authors suggest it is "highly probable that Powers was a member of a secret organization, such as the Eastern Star." Color photographs of both Powers quilts are included.

Wahlman, Maude S. <u>Signs and Symbols: African Images in African-American Quilts</u>. New York: Studio Books, 1993. See pages 64 – 67. Wahlman proposes her own theory that "southern Bible quilts… may also have been used as adult baptismal robes." She also states that she "believe(s) that Harriet Powers may have been a conjure-woman or an elder member of a Masonic lodge, or both." The known photograph of Powers, wearing an appliquéd apron, is one piece of evidence Wahlman uses to support this claim. Wahlman also introduces us to other African American quilters who have stitched Bible quilts, such as Lorraine Maham of Philadelphia and Nora Ezell of Alabama.

Walker, Alice. <u>In Search of Our Mothers' Gardens</u>. New York: Harcourt Brace Jovanovich, 1983. See pages 231–243. The title article originally appeared in *Ms.* Magazine in 1974. Walker writes: "… in the Smithsonian Institution in Washington, D.C., there hangs a quilt unlike any other in the world. In fanciful, inspired, and yet simple and identifiable figures, it portrays the story of the Crucifixion. It is considered rare, beyond price. Though it follows no known pattern of quilt-making, and though it is made of bits and pieces of worthless rags, it is obviously the work of a person of powerful imagination and deep spiritual feeling."

Wooster, Ann-Sargent. <u>Quiltmaking: The Modern Approach to a Traditional Craft</u>. New York: Drake Publishers, 1972. References to Powers are on pages 93– 95.

Magazines, Journals and Newsletter Articles

Adams, Dr. Monni. "Harriet Powers' Bible Quilts." The Clarion, Museum of American Folk Art, New York, Spring 1982, p. 43.

Benberry, Cuesta. "African American Quilts Paradigms of Black Diversity." International Review of African American Art, vol. 12, no. 3, 1995, pp. 31–37.

Davidson, Ruth. "In the Museums." Antiques, October 1965. The *Pictorial Quilt* is shown on page 538. The article announces the acquisition of the quilt by the Museum of Fine Arts, Boston. Davidson says of the quilt "If the inspiration is naïve, the sense of design revealed in these compartmented compositions is extraordinary; the creator of the quilt had not only a highly sophisticated color sense but, one feels, a delightful sense of humor."

"Department of Textiles." Annual Report 1964, Museum of Fine Arts, Boston. Formal notice that the *Pictorial Quilt* is officially part of the museum's collection as bequeathed by Maxim Karolik.

Elsley, Judy. "The Smithsonian Quilt Controversy: Cultural Dislocation." In Uncoverings 1993, edited by Laurel Horton, pp. 119–136. San Francisco: American Quilt Study Group, 1994. In-depth article where Elsley argues that the "Smithsonian Controversy represents a struggle over women's history, its place, purpose, and significance."

Fedde, Gerry. "The Quilt Craft of Harriet Powers." Ebony, Jr., March 1984, p. 13.

Gibbs, Eleanor C. "The Bible Quilt." Atlantic Monthly, July 1922, pp. 65 – 67. A fictional account of a slave washerwoman who describes her various quilts, including her favorite Bible quilt, to "Miss Mandy's little gal." This story is told in dialect and is horrible to read from my twenty-first-century perspective.

Hanna, Emily and Paula Eubanks. "Instructional Resource: Visual and Verbal Arts of the Akan and the Transmission to African-American Culture." Art Education, vol. 53, no. 2, March 2000, pp. 25–32. Harriet Powers' quilts are incorporated into an art lesson.

Jeffries, Rosalind. "African Retentions in African American Quilts and Artifacts." International Review of African American Art, vol. 11, no. 2, 1994, pp. 32–33.

Mason, Rhonda. "Daughters of Harriet Powers: A Tribute to an American Quiltmaker." Patchwork Quilts Magazine, October 1997, pp. 15–20. Includes text and photos of quilts by Ana Aruz, Virginia Harris, Peggy Hartwell, and Kyra Hicks.

McArdle, Kathleen A. "The Pictorial Quilts of Harriet Powers." School Arts, vol. 104, no. 6, February 2005. 3 pages. Instructions for creating cut-paper quilt blocks for storytelling.

McDaniel, M. Akua. "Black Women: Making Quilts of Their Own." Art Papers, September/October 1987.

Morgan, Julie and Karin Zipf. "Athens' African-American Heritage." Athens Magazine, June 1996, pp. 89–91, 94–95.

Mullen, Harryette. "African Signs and Spirit Writing." Callalo, vol. 19, no. 3, 1996, pp. 670–689. Includes discussion of Harriet Powers and her quilts.

"Out of Necessity: Harriet Powers Pieced Together Her African Continuity." About…Time, May 31, 1999, p. 40. Article about Harriet Powers on the occasion of her *Pictorial Quilt* being on display in Atlanta, Georgia as part of the *Georgia Quilts: Piecing Together History* exhibit.

Rybicki, Verena M. "Harriet Powers Heritage." Quilting International, November 1992, pp. 12–14. Summarizes the Powers story from the research of Marie Jeanne Adams and Gladys-Marie Fry.

Schraffenberger, Nancy. "Warmth for Body and Soul." Guideposts, October 1984, pp. 24–29. Harriet Powers' *Bible Quilt* is among the various religious-themed quilts shown in the article.

Shallcross, Gilian and Dorothy Amore Pilla. "Pictorial Quilt." School Arts, vol. 100, no. 5 January 2001, p. 39. Activities for classroom art projects based on the Powers quilts.

"Smithsonian Quilts." Spiegel Catalog, 1992. Full-page photograph of the *Bible Quilt* in mass reproduction. Twin ($198), full/queen ($298), king ($398), and standard size pillow sham ($59) were available for sale.

Stevenson, Amy Barton. "Smithsonian Quilt Collection." Quilter's Gallery Magazine, vol. 51, January 1974, pp. 4–5. Early article about the Harriet Powers *Bible Quilt*.

"Story-Telling Quilts: Tales Drawn in Thread." Quilt (magazine), Summer 1984, p. 30. Includes photo of a Bible quilt by Lucile Degangi. The quilt was displayed at the West Broward Quilters Guild Show in 1983. Degangi says she was inspired by Harriet Powers' quilt at the Smithsonian.

Terrace, Lisa C. "Appliqué Quilt." Bulletin (Museum of Fine Arts, Boston), vol. 62, 1964, pp. 162–163. This article is about the Harriet Powers *Pictorial Quilt*.

Troyen, Carol. "Maxim Karolik: Folk Art." Antiques, April 2001, pp. 588–599. Insightful biography about Karolik and the extraordinary collection of art he and his wife, Martha, gave to the Museum of Fine Arts, Boston. The *Pictorial Quilt* is one of the objects highlighted and featured on the magazine's cover.

Wahlman, Maude. "Religious Symbolism in African American Quilts." The Clarion (Museum of American Folk Art), vol. 14, no. 3, Summer 1989, pp. 36–43.

Wildemuth, Susan. "The Beautiful Bible Quilt: Telling the Story in Needle and Thread." Quilt Magazine, Spring 1998, pp. 50–51, 105. Article about Harriet Powers' two known quilts.

Newspapers

Biles, Jan. "Topekan Re-Creates History's Finest Quilts." The Topeka Capital Journal (KS), March 14, 2007. Hortense Horton Beck, eighty-seven years old, stitches reproductions of historical quilts. On display at the Metropolitan Arts Council Gallery in Greenville, South Carolina are eleven of Beck's historical quilts, including the *Pictorial Quilt*. The exhibit coincides with the premiere of *Quilting the Sun*, a play about Harriet Powers by Grace Cavalieri.

Bourne, Kay. "Intricate Quilts Weave Together Fabric of African American Life." The Bay State Banner (Boston, MA), November 10, 1994, vol. 30, issue 8, p. 18. The *Pictorial Quilt* is on display for the first time in five years in the textile exhibit *Sweet Dreams: Bedcovers and Bed Clothes*, curated by Marianne Carlanoa and Nicole J. Shiliam. The quilt is one of sixty items on display. Susan Thompson, of the African American Master Artist-in-Residency Program, is quoted in the article.

Bowen, Nancy Bunker. "American Tapestry: Story Quilts of Harriet Powers Reveal Remarkable Artistry." <u>Athens Banner-Herald</u> (GA), September 2, 2001. Extensive overview of Harriet Powers' life.

Cairns, Craig. "Quilts' Sale Revives Interest." <u>Chronicle-Tribune</u> (Marion, IN), July 24, 1995, p. A8. Cuesta Benberry presents lecture titled *America's Cherished Quilts: The Harriet Powers Bible Quilts.*

"Calendar." <u>Washington Post</u>, April 3, 1969, p. E8. Large photo of the *Bible Quilt.* "Harriett, an elderly Negro farm woman from the outskirts of Athens, GA, created this 'Bible Quilt'... It can be seen in the Recent Acquisition Exhibit on the First Floor of the Smithsonian's Museum of History and Technology."

Cillie, LaCheryl B. "Hidden Treasures–Harriet Powers, Quilter and Storyteller." <u>New Pittsburgh Courier</u>, February 17, 1999, p. C12. Part two of a two-part series syndicated to several U.S. newspapers.

Clayton, Richard. "Quilters Stitch Up a Benefit." <u>Columbian</u> (Vancouver, WA), November 27, 1999, p. B1. Local quilters raise funds for medical team through a second annual quilt auction. One highlighted auction item is a full-size reproduction of a Harriet Powers' quilt stitched by a group Clackamas, Oregon quilters.

"Colored Fair." <u>Atlanta Constitution</u> (GA), various dates 1886. This newspaper published a few articles related to the segregated fair held in Athens, Georgia weeks after the Northeast Georgia Fair of 1886 and on the same camp grounds. Harriet Powers exhibited the *Bible Quilt* at the Cotton Fair of 1886, presumably officially known as the Northeast Georgia Fair. The Atlanta Constitution articles included:

"To Give the Negroes a Chance." August 13, 1886, p. 2. The Northeast Georgia Fair Association gives approval "to the colored people" to hold a fair.

"Affairs About Athens." August 21, 1886, p. 2. The Colored Fair Association members are published: Madison Davis, president; Wesley Williams, vice-president; John Mack, treasurer; E. W. Brydie, W. H. Easlis, and R. S. Harris, secretaries; Noah Johnson, A. F. Hawkins, Emanuel Jenkins, R. H. Durham, Ed Aufling, G. H. Davis, Sr., and Samuel M. McQueen, executive committee members.

"The Colored Fair." November 21, 1886, p. 6. Notes the fair runs from Tuesday to Saturday. Horse racing will be featured event.

"The Colored Fair." November 23, 1886, p. 2. Notes J(udson). W. Lyons, a "colored lawyer" of Augusta, gave opening remarks at the Fair. The event opened "very creditably" to bad weather.

Lyons later serves as Register of the Treasury (1898–1906) and had his signature printed on all U.S. paper money during his tenure. To date five African Americans have had their signatures on US paper currency: Registers of the Treasury Blanche K. Bruce (1881–1885, 1897–1898), Lyons, William T. Vernon (1906–1911), James C. Napier (1911–1913), and Treasurer of the United States Azie Taylor Morton (1977–1981).

1899 Silver Dollar Bill, Signed by J. W. Lyons
Collection of the author

"The Colored Fair Successful." November 27, 1886, p. 2. The article noted that the "colored fair is a success financially, and will pay all expenses. There has been some good racing on the grounds the last few days."

Glueck, Grace. "The Art-Minded Have a Field Day." New York Times, February 17, 1990, p. 15. The College Art Association holds a four-day conference for its 78th annual convention. Mara R. Witzling of the University of New Hampshire compares one of Harriet Powers' quilt "to a work as highly positioned within the canon as Michelangelo's Sistine Chapel ceiling."

Glueck, Grace. "Expressions of Hope and Faith, Inspired by the Work of a Freed Slave." New York Times, January 30, 2004, p. E37. Art review of the quilt exhibition *Threads of Faith,* which featured Peggie Hartwell's quilt in honor of Harriet Powers.

Hammes, Mary Jessica. "Storytelling Festival Honors the Art of the Tale." Athens Banner-Herald (Athens, GA), March 7, 2002. First annual Stitching Stars Storytelling Festival is a day-long event featuring Bobby Norfolk, Sherry Norfolk and Andy Offutt Irwin. The name of the festival is inspired by the book Stitching Stars: The Story of Quilts of Harriet Powers by Mary E. Lyons.

"Handmade Quilts Reflect 19th Century Designs." Kansas City Star, January 3, 1992, p. E4. The Smithsonian's National Museum of American History sells reproduction of nineteenth-century quilts from its collection, including the *Bible Quilt* by Harriet Powers.

Hatfield, Julie. "Art of the Bedroom: Climbing for Cancer Fund; A Little Curl Talk." Boston Globe, January 16, 1995, Living, p. 45. *Sweet Dreams: Bedcovers and Bed Clothes* exhibit at the Museum of Fine Arts. A rare appliqué bedcover made by Harriet Powers is featured.

Hester, Conoly. "2 Searchers Find Quilt Maker Data." Athens Banner Herald, March 17, 1976, pp. 1, 12. Dr. Gladys-Marie Fry, sponsored by the Georgia Council for the Arts, researches courthouse tax rolls, deed records, and U.S. Census data in her quest to uncover details of Harriet Powers' life. Lovely photograph of Dr. Fry searching records in the University of Georgia Library is shown.

Hiskey, Michelle. "Historic Quilt a Feather in Atlanta's Cap." Atlanta Journal-Constitution, April 4, 1999, p. M1. Preview of *Georgia Quilts: Piecing Together a History* exhibit at the Atlanta History Center. Harriet Powers' *Pictorial Quilt* on temporary loan from the Boston Museum of Fine Art. Extensive 1,666 word article. Includes quotes by Anita Weinraub, co-curator of the *Georgia Quilts* exhibit. A quote by Doris Bowman, a thirty-five-year veteran of the Smithsonian, stands out. She spoke about the museum receiving the Harriet Powers *Bible Quilt.* Bowman says:

> "It just came in the mail and we opened it and we were just floored....It was so different from anything we had ever seen."

Hiskey, Michelle. "The Patchwork of a Family Treasure." Atlanta Journal-Constitution, April 4, 1999, p. M2. Interview and photo of Joe Carter, a descendent of Harriet Powers, shares how he felt in 1996 when he first saw a newspaper article showing distant relatives pictured in front of the *Pictorial Quilt* at the Museum of Fine Arts, Boston. Carter would then organize family members to see the *Bible Quilt* at the Smithsonian Museum of American History. Carter was "awestruck" that the *Pictorial Quilt* will be on display in Atlanta.

Holmes, Cat Mantione. "19th Century Artist Lives on Through 'Story' Quilts." Online Athens (GA), July 12, 1999. http://onlineathens.com/stories/071299/cla_cat.shtml [accessed May 10, 2008]. Two-page first-person account of seeing Harriet Powers' *Pictorial Quilt* on display at the Atlanta History Museum in the exhibit *Georgia Quilts: Piecing Together a History*.

Koncius, Jura. "Last Stitch in the *Smithsonian Quilt* Saga." Washington Post, March 21, 1996, p. T5. A rosewood quilt case, fitted with fiber-optic lighting and costing $13,000, was unveiled at the Smithsonian's National Museum of American History. The case is set to showcase historical quilts in the museum's collection.

Koncius, Jura. "Museum Quilts For the Home." Washington Post, December 26, 1991, p. T5. This may have been the first article the *Post* printed on what would become the Smithsonian Quilt Controversy. In less than 300 words, the reporter stated the Smithsonian Institution licensed about 600 products to generate $18 million in annual retail sales. The Smithsonian licensed designs of four 19th century quilts in its collection, including the *Bible Quilt*, to be made in China. The retail prices would range from $200 - $500. It was noted the quilts would cost $1,500 each if made in the U.S.

Koncius, Jura. "Patching Things Up." Washington Post, March 16, 1995, p. T5. Update on the Smithsonian Quilt Controversy and one outcome from discussions between the Institution and the American Quilt Defense Fund. The two groups had signed a memorandum of understanding to foster future study of American quiltmaking. Two-day quilt symposium planned for March 18–19, 1995 at the Smithsonian to discuss topics such as immigrant traditions within quilting and African American quiltmaking.

Koncius, Jura. "The Power, the Glory, the Quilts." Washington Post, March 11, 1993, p. T14. Extensive 3,665 word article. Focus is on the Cabin Creek Quilts, a West Virginia quiltmaking cooperative, which had delivered more than 100 quilts to Lands' End, a popular mail order catalog retailer. The quilts would sell for $800 each. The article outlined the challenges faced by the cooperative in the face of quilt imports. The article also indicated that American Pacific, the company the Smithsonian Institution licensed to reproduce selected nineteenth-century quilts, including the Harriet Powers' *Bible Quilt*, had "sold 23,000 of the Smithsonian designs."

Koncius, Jura. "The Quilts That Struck a Nerve: Smithsonian Reproductions Spark a Passionate Protest." Washington Post, March 19, 1992, p. T08. Many American quilters are horrified when handmade copies of historic Smithsonian nineteenth-century quilts appeared in a 1992 Spiegel catalog. In need of revenues, the Smithsonian Institution licensed the rights to reproduce items from its collection to a Chinese factory. Three reproduced quilts involved included Harriet Powers' 1886 *Bible Quilt*, a *Bride's Quilt* made in 1851 by a Carroll County bride, and a 1830 *Great Seal of the United States* quilt by Susan Strong, of Frederick County, Maryland. Pillow shams and small hooked rugs to match the reproduction quilts were also available. A fourth quilt design, a copy of an 1850 pattern called *Sunburst*, was introduced in a winter 1992 Chambers mail-order catalog. American quilters protested the historical quilts being reproduced and non-Americans producing the quilts. Viola Canady, founder of the Daughters and Sons of Dorcas, was quoted in the article. Then-Senator Al Gore (D-Tenn), Hazel Carter, Virginia Gunn, and other quilt enthusiasts are quoted.

Koncius, Jura. "The Smithsonian's Truce Imported Copies Spark Agreement–And A New Protest." Washington Post, March 25, 1993, p. T06. Karey Bresenhan and Nancy O'Bryant are scheduled to appear before the House Appropriations Subcommittee on the Interior and Related Agencies, which was set to review the Smithsonian's 1994 budget.

Leonard, Pamela Blume. "Visual Arts: Quilts Tell Story of Heart, Home." Atlanta Journal-Constitution, February 1, 2002, p. Q6. Review of the exhibit *Heart Melodies: African-American Quilts Made in Georgia* at the Spruill Center Gallery in Atlanta, Georgia. About thirty quilts are displayed, including Jessie Telfair's 1975 "Freedom Quilt" and a reproduction of a Harriet Powers quilt.

Link, Melissa. "Stitching Stars Storytelling Festival Has Tales to Tell." Athens Banner-Herald (Athens, GA), March 13, 2003. Jackie Elsner, Children's Librarian at the Athens-Clarke County (ACC) Library and Michael Bush, ACC Library Branch Manager, co-coordinated the first storytelling festival the previous year.

Loercher, Diana. "Two Centuries of Black Pioneers in American Art." Christian Science Monitor, July 16, 1976, p. 23. Review of the exhibit "Selections of Nineteenth Century Afro-American Art." Included in the show was the *Pictorial Quilt*.

Lyons, Mary E. "American Quilt: Dropped Stitch." New York Times, November 5, 1995. In a Letter to the Editor, Lyons protests a previous *New York Times* review of the movie "How To Make An American Quilt" as well as the book for not acknowledging that the storyline is, in part, derived from the life of Harriet Powers.

Negip, Judith A. "Quilt with Tales to Tell Comes to MFA." The Bay State Banner (Boston, MA), September 22, 1994, vol. 30, issue 1, p. 4b. The *Pictorial Quilt* is displayed in the newly renovated Textile Gallery from Oct 21, 1994 to March 12, 1995. The article does not mention other items on display. Assuming this is the *Sweet Dreams* exhibit.

"Northeast Georgia Fair." Atlanta Constitution, November 10, 1886, p. 2. The fair opens to a "good crowd." Fair attendants are "coming in on every train." The Fair is most likely the "Cotton Fair of 1886" held in Athens, Georgia in which Jennie Smith first saw Harriet Powers' *Bible Quilt* on display.

"Northeast Georgia Fair." Atlanta Journal, various dates 1886. This newspaper published daily special notices from Athens, Georgia. The reporter's byline for each is "B. H. N," unless otherwise noted. It is likely this fair is the 1886 Cotton Fair that Jennie Smith refers to in her description of first seeing Harriet Powers' *Bible Quilt*.

November 10, 1886, Wednesday, p. 1. "The second day of the Northeast Georgia Fair opened with a much larger attendance than yesterday. The weather is superb. The outlook for the fair is highly encouraging. The trotting and pacing races are attracting great attention..."

November 11, 1886, p. 1. "Immense attention to-day; cattle show fine. The premium for the largest yield of corn to the acre was awarded to M. L. Branch, of Oconee..."

November 12, 1886, p. 1. "The Northeast Georgia Fair improves daily. The art display and mercantile exhibits compare very favorably with that of the late State exposition. Special mention must be made of the superb display of jellies, preserves, pickles and canned fruits, by Mrs. I. W. Lucas, of Athens. It surpasses anything of the kind seen at a Georgia fair in years. Other displays by the ladies will be touched later, for they richly deserve it..."

November 13, 1886, p.1. by W. H. P. "The fair, which has been talked about and written about for some weeks, opened here auspiciously on Tuesday morning, and the attendance since the opening has been very fine. To-day's exercises were especially well attended on account of the extra attractions – the base ball game between the University and Town nines, and the presence of the Lucy Cobb Institute young Ladies. A feature of the fair which is quite popular is the exhibit of poultry and live stock.

"The favorite spot with all was the ladies' department, where the beauty of the collection showed the skill of the fair exhibitors with both needle and stove. Mrs. Prof. White, of Athens, and many others had ornamental work that was greatly admired. The collection of paintings and ornamental china, by Miss. Sosnowasi [spelling unclear on microfilm], of the Horne school, was a tribute to the well known skills of this popular instructress...."

November 13, 1886, p. 1. "A Brilliant Success. The patronage being given the Northeast Georgia fair is agreeably surprising. Fully three thousand people entered the gates Friday. Without disparagement the following displays deserve special notice: ... In the art department, the collection of paintings on canvas and china by pupils of the Horne school and the Lucy Cobb Institute cannot be surpassed.

"Specimens of Kensington embroidery by Miss. Lucy Hull, of Savannah, attracted great attention. The display of china painting by Mrs. J. H. Fleming, of Athens, is both beautiful and extensive. Mr. J. C. Hutchins shows some splendid lace and fancy work...

"The premium for the best bale of cotton was awarded Robert Iverson, of Athens..."

November 15, 1886, p. 1. "Rain prevented a large assemblage at the Northeast Georgia fair to-day. Those present, though, were highly entertained with some good racing... The balance of the premiums were decided upon to-day, and to-morrow they will be awarded... A handsomely made shirt by Mrs. John H. Newton, of Athens, a lady of 85 years, deserves special note...President W. B. Toomas, of the Fair Association, has done everything to make the exhibition a success, and, with the aid of such very efficient officers as Secretary W. D. Griffeth and Assistant Secretary W. S. Morris, has admirably accomplished it.

"The organ recital to-night at the Lucy Cobb Institute was highly entertaining. It took place in the Seney-Stoval chapel, before a cultured audience..."

Rogers, Patricia Dane. "A Bible of Black History." Washington Post, March 19, 1992, p. T08. Some quilters are outraged to learn that the Smithsonian will make Harriet Power's *Bible Quilt* available as a made-in-China reproduction.

Rogers, Patricia Dane. "Quilters' Protest Answered: Smithsonian Agrees to Label Imports." Washington Post, April 11, 1992, p. G01. Smithsonian responds to protests against the licensing of four of its antique American quilts for reproduction in China. Harriet Powers' 1886 *Bible Quilt* is one of the quilts. Fifteen "high-profile" individuals representing quilters nationally meet with Roger Kennedy, director of the National Museum of American History, to insist the Smithsonian cancel its contract to reproduce quilts from its collection. The Smithsonian resists, but it does agree to label the reproduced quilts as "Made in China."

Russell, John. "Gallery View: Discovering Afro-American Art From the 19th Century." New York Times, June 27, 1976, p. 76. Art critic review of the "Selections of 19th Century Afro American Art" exhibit at the Metropolitan Museum of Art. Of Harriet Powers, Russell writes "the force of her imagination that she never failed to produce just the ideogram that stays with us long after we have walked down the Great Staircase of the Met and gone home." Includes photo of the *Pictorial Quilt*.

Sanderlin, Phil. "Quilting Party: $$ for Botanical Garden." The photocopy of this article sent to me by the Athens-Clarke County Library does not have any source data. My best guess is that the newspaper is the Athens Observer (GA), where Phil Sanderlin worked for twenty-six years before his death in June 2001. The article is about an upcoming fundraiser for the University of Georgia Botanical Garden by the Friends of the University of Georgia Botanical Garden on September 21 (year unknown, but likely 1981 or 1984). One of the fundraising prizes was a replica of the Harriet Powers *Pictorial Quilt*. According to the article, Drs. Vicki and Gerry Fedde of Durham, North Carolina began the replica and were assisted by Mary Abney, Linda Anderson, Elizabeth Powell, Diane Penny Wilson, JoAnn Yates, and Maureen O'Brien of Athens, Georgia. Others who participated included Jean Frett of Texas and Sherri Means of Richmond, Virginia. Additional paperwork from the Athens-Clarke County Library lists others who also participated in the creation of the replica quilt from 1980–1981 as Betty Belanger, Ruth Bryson, Catherine Craig, Dorothy Keach, and Dori Porter. Mrs. Pauline Hartford gave a 1984 replica quilt made by these same women to the Athens-Clarke County Library in March 2002 in honor of the First Annual Stitching Stars Storytelling Festival. The quilt, along with a commemorative plaque, is still on display today as of January 2009 in the main staircase at the Athens-Clarke County Library, 2025 Baxter Street, Athens, GA 30606. www.clarke.public.lib.ga.us.

Starrs, Chris J. "Stories For All." Athens Banner-Herald (Athens, GA), January 5, 2006. Fifth annual Stitching Stars Storytelling Festival in Athens, Georgia. Jackie Elsner, children's librarian at the Athens-Clarke County Library and one of the festival organizers, is quoted as saying the location for the festival "at the Seney-Stovall Chapel, where an art teacher from the nearby Lucy Cobb Institute purchased one of the quilts."

Temin, Christine. "MFA Shows Off Its Textile Treasures." Boston Globe, August 20, 1980, p.1. The exhibit "From Fiber To Fine Arts" opens. The critic explains that fiber is the only thread gliding through the show. "Thus, a quilt stitched by a 19th century black American, Harriet Powers, with an energetic jumble of characters including a Noah's Ark pair of elephants bumping heads, hangs next to an exquisite 17th century French silk damask table cloth…"

Trescott, Jacqueline. "Portraits of the Past." Washington Post, July 12, 1976, p. B1. Review of the exhibit *Selections of Nineteenth Century Afro-American Art* at the Metropolitan Museum of Art. Of the

Powers' *Pictorial Quilt*, Trescott writes the quilt "affirms that the artistic imagination flourishes under the most adverse conditions." Trescott interviews Reginia A. Perry, who organized the show. New York artist Benny Andrews, co-founder of the Black Emergency Cultural Coalition, was critical of the show. Andrews was quoted as saying, "It appears that the Metropolitan is so willing to give credence to an art style that is so traditional. Making it only 19th century, without any parallels to the conditions of the time, makes it very unsettling, even surreal."

Wakelyn, Catherine. "Disappearing American Tradition." Washington Post, March 29, 1992, Letter to the Editor, p. C06. Wakelyn, a former quilter, is pleased with the Smithsonian's decision to reproduce quilts from its collection as a means to "increase the public's appreciation of them."

Ward, Taylor. "Stitching a Story." St. Petersburg Times, February 21, 1997, p.8. *Daughters of Harriet Powers: Tribute to an American Quiltmaker* exhibit review.

Williams, Lena. "Foreign Competition for an American Art: Quilting." New York Times, January 14, 1993. Detailed article that includes quotes from Nadine Block, a founder of American Pacific, the vendor selected to manufacture the Smithsonian reproduction quilts, including the *Bible Quilt*.

Dissertations, Theses, Manuscripts and Papers

Barrow, Phyllis Jenkins. A History of Lucy Cobb Institute. Master's thesis, University of Georgia, 1951. Includes insights about Jennie Smith, who purchased Harriet Powers' *Bible Quilt*.

Brooks, Cheryl Melody. Nineteenth and early Twentieth Century African American Women's Quilt-Making: A Communicative Perspective. Master's thesis, Howard University, 1997. A copy is available from the Moreland-Spingarn Research Center at Howard University.

Coleman, Janice. Meditating Upon Means: The Black Seamstress in Nineteenth Century American Literature. Ph.D Diss. University of Mississippi, 1998, 146 pages. UMI number: 9921126.

Grace Cavalieri papers, 1955-2008, Special Collections Research Center, The George Washington University, Washington, DC 20052. Phone:

(202) 994–7549. MS2007. 73 linear feet. There are several draft manuscripts for projects related to Harriet Powers' life story:

- Quilting the Sun by Grace Cavalieri. Box 26, Folder 5
- Amidst the Seven Stars, 1991. Box 30, Folders 1–7
- Anything for Wisement, 1991. Box 30, Folder 8
- Jennie and the Jujuman, 2004. Box 32, Folder 3
- Mrs. Powers and Miss Smith, various dates, Boxes 32, 33

Julia Neely Finch Papers, 1890–1926, W.S. Hoole Special Collections Library, The University of Alabama. 0.8 linear feet. Collection of correspondence, poetry, short stories, newspaper clippings, and photographs. Includes letters to and from her daughter, Lucine Finch.

Lucine Finch Manuscripts, Birmingham Public Library, Department of Archives and Manuscript. 1 Box. Includes two-page bibliography of Finch, a five-page short story titled *The Darkey and the Deed: A (nig) Heroic Tale* by Finch, and a fifty-eight page story titled *Mammy's Past Crust* by her mother, Julia Neely Finch.

Frey, Valerie Janese. North Georgia Folk Art: A Model Curriculum for the Fourth Grade. Applied Project Report as Partial Fulfillment for Masters of Art Education degree. University of Georgia, Athens, 1995. Lesson eight focuses on Harriet Powers and planning and creating a paper quilt.

Karolik-Codman Family Papers 1714—1964. Massachusetts Historical Society, 1154 Boylston Street, Boston, MA 02215-3695. Phone: (617) 536-1608. More than 32 boxes, 34 volumes, offsite reel-to-reel storage. MS N-2164. Twenty page Finding Aid available online. Of particular interest is the Maxim Karolik and Martha Codman Karolik papers, 1881—1964. The Maxim Karolik papers include letters between Karolik and various private art dealers, art historians, cultural institutions and museums; writings and lectures; financial papers; concert programs and announcements; newspaper clippings; and sound recordings. Correspondence about the purchase of the *Pictorial Quilt* is located here. It is unclear whether any other documents about the quilt are also located here. There are at least eighteen paintings and drawings with definite or likely African American imagery in the collective M. and M. Karolik Collections. I'd love to see if any records indicate what prices were paid for these images and how those prices compare to the *Pictorial Quilt*!

Larson, Judy Lorraine. Three Southern Fairs. Ph.D Diss. Emory University, 1998. 492 pages. UMI number: 9901860. Larson provides in-depth insights into the Cotton States and International Exposition, Atlanta; 1895 Tennessee Centennial, Nashville; 1897 South Carolina Inter-State and the West Indian Exposition, Charleston, 1901–1902. Of particular interest are the appendices. Appendix A outlines "Fair Facts" from each event. Appendix B provides many of the names of the visual artists displayed at the three fairs. Appendix D section titled "African American Artists/Artisans at All Three Fairs." Harriet Powers' *Bible Quilt* was displayed at the 1895 Atlanta Cotton Exposition. Larson includes an image of the quilt on display. Jennie Smith exhibited a panel of painted roses as part of the Lucy Cobb Institute display in the Women's Building (page 398).

Lester, Jody. Cut From the Same Cloth: Power, Property, and the Politics of Preservation. Master's thesis, Yale University, 1991. Includes biography of Harriet Power and interpretation of the *Pictorial Quilt*. Because the Museum of Fine Arts, Boston restricts access to the quilt when it is not on display, Lester analyzed the quilt via a set of slides. Lester is a quilter. The chapters in her thesis include: 1) Designs on Power: Harriet Powers' Quilt and the Politics of Preservation; 2) Cultural Motifs: Interpretation of a slide; 3) Patterns of Hegemony: Harriet Powers as Object 1837–1865; and 4) Historical Appliqué: the Relationship of the Slide to Powers as Object.

Schinkel, Peter Evans. The Negro in Athens and Clarke County, 1872 – 1900. Master's thesis, University of Georgia, Athens, 1971. Chapter titles include Work and Property, Religious and Social Life, Education, Crime and Punishment, and Race Relations in Politics. Excellent background material.

Simpson, Yaalieth Adrienne. African-American Female Identity in the 19th Century: The Individual and Cultural Empowerment of Harriet Powers' Bible Quilts. Ph.D Diss. Teachers College, Columbia University, 2003. 213 pages. UMI number 3091295. Examines Powers' life and quiltmaking via sociologist Patricia Hill Collins' theory of empowerment.

Smith/Finch Family Papers. Birmingham-Jefferson History Museum, Birmingham, Alabama. Donated items from the family of Alice Finch Smith and Lucine Finch. Alice was the daughter of Edwin W.

Finch, Jr., one of Lucine's brothers. It is unclear whether the Family Papers include any references to Harriet Powers' *Bible Quilt*.

Jennie Smith Papers. Hargrett Rare Book & Manuscript Library, University of Georgia Libraries, Athens, GA 30602. Phone: (706) 542-7123. 1.5 linear ft. Five boxes, one oversize folio of drawings. MSS 13. Two page Finding Aid for the content of each box is available. According to a May 29, 2009 email to the author from the Library, Jennie Smith donated a set of materials in 1943, then a bequest from her estate came in 1946, and Mr. and Mrs. Harold Heckman donated additional materials in 1960, 1961 and 1964.

According to the library's website: "The collection consists of the personal papers of Jennie Smith from 1863-1944. Includes correspondence (1883-1944), clippings, sketches, printed pictures, engravings, drawings, designs for art contests, pages from *Godey's Lady's Book* and *Frank Leslies Magazine*, photographs, notebooks, and a diary of Jennie Smith." The diary had been closed by order of Mr. and Mrs. Harold Heckman until 2000 – more than fifty years after Smith passed away. There doesn't appear to be any reference to Harriet Powers, the *Bible Quilt* or the *Pictorial Quilt* in the Papers.

Other memorable items include Smith's obituary, biography, lovely photographs of her home on the Lucy Cobb Institute campus, a unique 3D-like structure of the Institute Smith appears to have created, and a dozen issues of *The Athens Republique*, the local African American newspaper, dated from 1922 to 1926. The newspapers include local church and lodge directories. The Papers also include several colored drawings of items related to the Atlanta Cotton Exposition. Jennie Smith must have also been a naturist, as her Papers includes a piece of an actual squirrel's tail!

Young-Minor, Ethel A. "To Redeem Her Body": Performing Womanist Liberation (Zora Neale Hurston, May Miller, Ntozake Shange, Anna Deavere Smith). Ph.D Diss. Bowling Green State University 1997. This study is "a reconsideration of African American female voices in performance." Harriet Powers' *Bible Quilt* is one of the objects used to demonstrate a voice in performance. AAG9820930.

Plays and Poems

Cavalieri, Grace. <u>Quilting the Sun</u>. A fictional play based on the life of Harriet Powers. The script took poet and playwright Cavalieri ten years to complete. In a March 2008 email to this author, she said:

> "My task was to imagine reasons Harriet might have sold her quilt. It was her lifelong project and, after all, she had always lived in poverty. Why did she need money at this particular time, and need it so badly that she relinquished a "spelled quilt," one that (I imagined) God told her to make? The only reason I could believe was that she did it to save the life of her child. Essentially, she sold one baby for another."

In March 2003 *Quilting the Sun* was presented at the Smithsonian Institution. Shela Xoregos, director.

Cast:

Gregory Ward	Narrator
Denise Lock	Harriet Powers
Eric Coleman	Armsted Powers
Christine Karl	Jennie Smith
Christophe Dietz	Alonzo Powers
Rodney Sheley	Ju-ju Man/Uncle Jerry
Jean Richards	Millie Rutherford
Matthew Johnson	Jonathan Crawford
Dorthi Fox	Big Mama
Kim Gainer	Laura

In February 2007 the play premiered at the Centre Stage – South Carolina in Greenville. Carrie Ann Collins, director.

Cast:

Vallery Sledge	Harriet Powers
Seldon Peden	Armsted Powers
Lisa Justice	Jennie Smith
Tyson Malik Neal	Alonzo Powers
Willie J. Stratford, Jr.	Ju-ju Man/Uncle Jerry
Jean E Bartlett	Millie Rutherford
Anthony Goodin	Johnathan Crawford
Yvonne S. Reeder	Big Mama
Yolanda L. McRae	Laura

For more information about the play, visit www.gracecavalieri.com.

Harriet's Power
By Terri L. Jewell

The white ladies took her quilts as husbands.
                    Harriet neither read
                    nor wrote a sound
                    but remembered well
dreams from the Fon of Abomey,
mad dash of old sow Betts,
fables tendered in heaven –
                    the dark days
                    the one red night.
The patrons misread her age by twenty years.
                    They neither asked
                    nor cared to know
bondswoman, wife unattended
as they lined up graveside
swept of flagrant scraps of cloth,
                    worms of stray thread
                    felled by her scissors.
They carried off kudos Harriet had stitched,
                    each cryptic square
                    an eye jaundiced
                    to those radiant colors
pricked by her needle skilled
to lift into delivered flight
the offspring of Harriet's brain.

Terri L. Jewell (1954—1995) was born in Louisville, Kentucky. She was the editor of *The Black Woman's Gumbo Ya Ya*. Her poetry, essays, and other writings appeared in *African American Review, The Black Scholar, Calyx,* and other publications. The Terri L. Jewell Papers (MS 220) are located in the Michigan State University Library, Special Collections department. The poem *Harriet's Power* is reprinted with permission from her mother, Mrs. Mildred Jewell.

To My Mother, Harriet Powers
By Faylita Hicks

Oh Mother,
With needles for fingers.
Thread for hair.
Stitches for kisses.

I can still hear you praying.
Murmuring and crying over me,
Soaking my cheeks with your stories.
So many to tell, so many to remember.
You and God stitching me together,
As if I was made in your womb.

Here, mother, here is the blue
to make a man, God's man.
And here is the missus ripped
summer dress for the angels.
Take this scrap too, for the woman,
God's woman, like you.

A red bow for the blood of Cain
Old sheets for the animals of Adam.
Here is the needle and here is the thread.
I know you're tired, I know.

The moon will soon chase the sun out and
the day will be full of more stitching.
Curtains for the kitchen and clothes for the
missus' children.

Bits and pieces for your own sons and
daughters, but that will have to wait for
tomorrow.

Stitching together the nickels and dimes for
your land, the hole left in your heart by that
man. Stitching together your life the best
way you can. I know you're tired, I know.

But tonight Mother, kiss me by candle light.
Stitch me by moonlight, by the Northern
Star. We both know Freedom is not so far.

Stitch, stitch, stitch this slave's soul back
together, to be sold, you already know, it is
my destiny. Close your eyes now, I'll guide
your hands.

I know your secrets, my Maker, my Mother.
Let me soak up your tears and cover your
scars.

Here is the potato sack for the stars.
Here are the scraps for the stairs to heaven.
Here, the scrap from the pastor's ripped coat
for the Fallen Angel. It's only right he
should serve a higher purpose.

Now, border me in Eden, flower scraps from
the table cloth. The table too good for you,
is it true?

Pray into me, Mother. Bind me in ancient
rights and signs and stars and crooked lines
and know that I may be many things.

Maybe I'll be *your* map to freedom, your
glimpse into God's kingdom. Maybe I'll be
the *way to* remember the sacrifice of your
callused fingers every December. Maybe I'll
be a way to ensure the *survival* of your
children.

Cook me in the kettle then.
Get all this dust off me, I'm ready.

Wrap me, a coat of many colors, around
your shoulders.

Wrap me around your children.
Sing me to rest atop their bodies.

Chant me an old hymn.
So that when the time comes, you can barter
my back, patch by worn patch, proudly.
Again and again.

This was always my purpose, you know.

Don't worry Mother, for God's watchful eye
rests on you and His merciful hand caresses
my back.

Oh Mother,
With needles for fingers.
Thread for hair.
Stitches for kisses.

No matter the years lost, faded.
No matter the great forfeit.
I am and always shall be yours.

Faylita Hicks is a spoken word artist, actress, and student at Texas State University - San Marcos. In 2007, Faylita released her first spoken word CD, *The Experience of This Black Woman*. This poem is reprinted with the poet's permission.

Bible Quilt, circa 1900
By Jane Wilson Joyce

Harriet Powers
stitched the Scripture
as she saw it.

With the joyful animals
dancing in the dawn
of the newmade world, she put
the independent hog
that ran five hundred miles
from Georgia to Virginia.
Her name was Betts.

With Adam and Eve,
the Falling of the Stars
in 1833. With Jonah and Moses,
Cold Thursday
when the bluebirds died,
and a woman froze
praying at her gate,
and a mule's breath
fell to icicles.

Christ crucified,
Mary and Martha weeping.

May 19, 1780
when the sun went off
to darkness,
the seven stars
were seen at noon,
the cattle went to bed,
the chickens to roost,
and in that Dark Day
a trumpet sounded.

Everywhere
the unwinking eye
of God, the merciful
hand outspread.

        *

Owing
to the hardness of the times,
Harriet Powers
asked ten dollars for that quilt.

Owing to the hardness of the times,
she took
five.

Handed it over
to Jennie Smith
wrapped in two sacks
like a baby; like a mother,
a slave mother,
Harriet slipped away to visit
her quilt. She was
'only in some measure consoled'
by the white woman's promise of
scraps.

Jane Wilson Joyce (b. 1947) is a professor of classics at Centre College in Danville, Kentucky. She is the author of *Beyond the Blue Mountains* (Gnomon Press, 1992) and *The Quilt Poems* (Mill Springs Press, 1984). This poem is reprinted with the poet's permission.

We Call Your Name, Harriet Powers
By Terri Lynne Singleton

We call your name, Harriet Powers:

two of your five children, born not of your womb, but of your hands, imagination, heart. Stitched as you lived under slavery, one later sold away from you, traveling in your lap, in my flour sack covering. Moving to the home and hands of Jennie Smith in 1890.

We call your name, Harriet Powers:

unable to read or write, you communicate through us of your visual and oral world. A world of the Bible and legends. A universe of the stars and the heavens. We speak for you, of the serpent in the Garden of Eden, Adam's rib, comets, eclipses, the sun, the God you have adopted as your own.

We call your name, Harriet Powers:

living in two museums, the Smithsonian in Washington, D.C., and the Museum of Fine Arts, Boston; we are among the chosen from the Smithsonian quilt collection. Manufactured in China. Quilts and pillow shams based on our faces, sold again in the marketplace. Accompanied by information stating our birth and where we live, neglecting your personal history and name.

We call your name, Harriet Powers:

that those who prosper from the labor of your hand and heart and those who rest upon and under your creativity shall know.

We call your name, Harriet Powers:

across the galleries and halls of the buildings in which we live –

across the farmland in the Buck Branch, Georgia, where you died,
free, in the year 1910 –

across the fields of the plantation you were born to, in 1837 and
on which you toiled till the end of the Civil War –

across the vast oceans to the homeland of your ancestors –

we call you home –

we call that others may hear –

we call your name –

Harriet Powers

Harriet Powers

Harriet Powers

Terri Lynne Singleton is a writer, filmmaker, event planner, and world traveler. She is the founder of Globalmix Films and the CEO of Concierge Design Group, both based in Louisville, Kentucky. This poem is reprinted with the poet's permission.

Videos, Storytelling, Art and Interactive Media

Annual Stitching Stars Storytelling Festival. Sixth annual event in 2007 sponsored by the Athens-Clarke (GA) County Library, 2025 Baxter Street, Athens, GA 30606, (706) 613-3650.

Barnett, Ivan. Harriet Powers II Collection mobile. I first saw a mobile inspired by the appliquéd pieces in the *Bible Quilt* while visiting with Mrs. Katharine Hall Preston in May 2008. I asked the artist, Ivan Barnett, at his Patina Gallery in Santa Fe, New Mexico about his Collection. In an April 17, 2009 email, Mr. Barnett responded:

> "I began seriously making art in the 1970s. Up until I saw the Harriet Powers quilt in Washington, my primary influences and focus was the folk art created by the Penna, Germans in the 18th and 19th centuries.
>
> "Seeing the Harriet Powers' quilt was somewhat of a turning point for me in my work. Her ability to design amazingly sophisticated shapes, and construct them in the form of a quilt, took my breath away. The abstract story telling aspect of her works inspired me greatly at the time. It was then that I decided to pay homage to Harriet by adapting some of her cutouts or shapes into contemporary works using the medium of my choice...thin steel. I recall making a series of mobiles, and perhaps other objects (mirrors, garden sculptures, and collages) starting in the early 1980s. Now 30 plus years later, I'm still paying homage to Harriet, by using some of the shapes she used in her quilts, in my current works. Thank you Harriet for paving the way, for me, toward abstract story telling. You helped give me permission to go further, as a young artist, all without a day of art school."

Botsford, Antoinette. "Talking Quilts, Hidden Stories: The Bible Quilts of Harriet Powers." Storyteller, Eastsound, WA.

Brooks, Joan Halimah. "A Stitch Back in Time." Real to Reel, March 10, 1996 segment. Brooks (1950–2003), a descendant of Harriet Powers via Charles H. Powers, hosted a five minute segment showing her Springfield, Massachusetts family seeing the *Pictorial Quilt* in person for the first time. The segment was taped on February 19, 1996. Those interviewed included: Dr. William H. Gilcher and great-grandchildren of Harriet Powers: Oscar Powers, Daisy Powers, and LaPheris Powers. There is a lovely image of the family's Bible with the names of family members recorded inside, including Harriet

Powers' name. Real to Reel is a television news magazine show produced by the Springfield (MA) Diocese and aired on NBC affiliate WWLP-22. For information on obtaining a copy of the segment, contact Catholic Communications, 65 Elliot Street, Springfield, MA 01107. Phone (413) 452-0686.

Heiser, Steve (Director). Missing Pieces: Contemporary Georgia Folk Art. 28 minutes. Portland, OR: Odyssey Productions for the Georgia Council for the Arts and Humanities, 1976. Includes references to the two known Harriet Powers quilts.

Hicks, Kyra. 2008. Harriet Powers Bible Quilt at the Air & Space Museum in DC [online]. Available from the World Wide Web on YouTube: http://www.youtube.com/watch?v=WZKwP7W9Op8. 2:48 minutes. This video features Harriet Powers' Bible Quilt in the "Treasures of American History" exhibit at the Smithsonian Air & Space Museum and was filmed one week before the exhibit ended.

Hicks, Kyra. 2008. Harriet Powers (1837 - 1910), African American Quilter Google Map [online]. Available from the World Wide Web on Google: http://maps.google.com. Type in the Search Box "Harriet Powers." This map pinpoints more than thirty significant locations from this book, such as Powers' hometown, exhibitions sites, and more! Click on any of the blue pushpins and read more about the locations. You can rate the map and leave your own comments.

Harriet Powers Map – Available on Maps.Google.com

Books or Magazines with a Powers Quilt on the Cover

Ackerman, James Stokes, Thayer S. Warshaw, and John Sweet. The Bible as/in Literature. Glenview, IL: Scott, Foresman, 1976. The first edition has the *Pictorial Quilt* on the cover. Beautiful!

Bateson, Mary Catherine. Full Circles, Overlapping Lives: Culture and Generation in Transition. New York: Random House, 2000. The paperback edition has the *Pictorial Quilt* on the cover.

Nichols, Catherine. African American Culture. Discovering the Arts. Vero Beach, FL: Rourke, 2006. Forty-eight page children's book. Features the *Pictorial Quilt* on the cover.

Poplack, Shana. The English History of African American English. Malden, MA: Blackwell Publishers, 1999. Features the *Pictorial Quilt* on the cover.

This April 2001 issue of Antiques magazine includes an extensive profile of Maxim Karolik, who bequeathed the *Pictorial Quilt* to the Museum of Fine Arts, Boston. (Courtesy Brant Publications, Inc.)

Ode to Harriet Powers by **Peggie Hartwell**
1995, 42 in. x 48 in.
Photograph by Karen Bell. Reprinted with the quilter's permission.
Visit www.PeggieHartwell.com

Harriet Powers: A Darling Offspring of Her Brain
by Marlene O'Bryant-Seabrook
1995, 69 in. x 92 in.
Visit www.MarleneOBryantSeabrook.com
Reprinted with the quilter's permission.

Smithsonian *Bible Quilt* reproduction and pillow sham
Collection of the author, purchased on eBay.com

Timeline

This timeline brings together significant events in the life of Harriet Powers and the people who have had contact with her or her quilts, exhibition dates for her two known quilts, and other interesting historical markers.

1830 – 1859

1837   Harriet Powers, the honored "Mother" of African American quilting, is born a slave in Georgia on October 29. In the Clarke County State of Georgia Returns and Mixed Records Book AA 1868–1884, page 33 is the full name of Powers:

Harriett Angeline Powers

1850   Harriet Beecher Stowe's *Uncle Tom's Cabin* is serialized in *National Era*, an abolitionist magazine.

1851   Sojourner Truth delivers her *Ain't I A Woman* speech at the National Women's Suffrage Convention in Akron, OH.

The Singer Sewing machine is introduced.

1852   *Uncle Tom's Cabin* is published in book form and sold 300,000 copies in its first year.

1854   *Carte-de-visite* photography is introduced in Paris.

1855   Harriet marries Armsted Powers.

1857   The U.S. Supreme Court rules in the *Dred Scott* case African Americans, whether slave or not, are not citizens of the United States and could never become citizens.

1858   The Lucy Cobb Institute is founded as a finishing school for young Southern women. Jennie Smith would teach there.

1860 – 1899

1861   The Civil War begins.

1862   Onieta Virginia "Jennie" Smith is born in Athens, Georgia. She would later purchase the *Bible Quilt* from Harriet Powers.

President Abraham Lincoln issues the Emancipation Proclamation declaring slaves in all Confederate states, including Georgia, to be free as of January 1, 1863.

1865   The Civil War ends.

1869   Henri Matisse, a leading French modern artist, is born.

1870   The U.S. Census lists Harriet Powers, her husband Armsted, and three children (Amanda, Leonzoe/Alonzo, Nancy). The record indicates that Harriet Powers cannot read or write.

1872   Harriet Powers "made a quilt of 4 thousand and 50 diamonds," according to a letter she wrote to Lorene Diver.

1874   Harriet purchases a Singer sewing machine (Source: Holmes, *Georgia Quilts*, page 180).

1879   The *Athens Blade* newspaper, featuring African American religious and social news, is founded in Athens. It ceased publication about 1884.

1880   Jennie Smith graduates from the Lucy Cobb Institute and begins to teach art there.

        The U.S. Census lists Harriet Powers, her husband Armsted, and three children (Alonzo, Lizzie, Marshall). The family is listed as Powell, not Powers. This census indicates that Harriet and her son, Alonzo, *can*, indeed, read and write.

1881   Alonzo Powers marries Julia Jackson in Clarke County, Georgia.

1882   The Gospel Pilgrim Cemetery, primarily for African Americans, is founded in Athens.

        Harriet Powers joins the Mt. Zion Baptist Church, according to a letter she wrote. There she "visited Sunday school and read the Bible more than ever. Then ... composed a quilt of the Lord's Supper from the New Testament. 2 thousand and 500 diamonds."

1886   Harriet Powers and her family move to Athens, Georgia.

        Harriet Powers' *Bible Quilt* exhibits at the Cotton Fair, most likely the Northeast Georgia Fair held November 9–13, in Athens.

        Jennie Smith, who wrote the Cotton Fair included a "Wild West Show, two Cotton Weddings and a circus," sees the quilt during the Fair, maybe displayed in a crafts area, and searches for the quiltmaker. On meeting Powers, Smith offers to purchase the quilt for $10. Powers refuses. The purchasing power of $10 during 1886 is worth $236 in 2008 dollars, according to MeasuringWorth.com.

Jennie Smith wins a prize for her artwork at the Fair. The local newspaper publishes an article about Smith's artwork at the Fair. The following week, her only surviving sibling, Wales Wynton, unexpectedly dies.

The Colored Fair is held on the same Athens fair grounds from November 22–27. Prominent African American and Augusta, Georgia lawyer Judson W. Lyons gives the opening speech. Lyons later serves as Register of the Treasury (1898–1906). His signature is printed on all U.S. paper currency during his tenure.

It is unclear whether Harriet Powers attended the Fair, heard J. W. Lyons speak, or had one or more of her quilts displayed at this Colored Fair of Athens.

1887   S. B. Davis begins editing the *Athens Clipper*, an African American weekly, four-page newspaper featuring religious and local events in Athens. Davis continues as editor for at least twenty years.

The Northeast Georgia Colored Fair Association hosts its second annual fair in Athens. The local newspaper reports that "[q]uilts, hand-made, of all descriptions, show a great deal of ingenuity, also a very large one, representing the crucifix;… always has a large crowd around it."

Harriet Powers "represented the star quilt in the colored fair association of Athens" and was awarded a "premium," according to a letter she wrote in 1896.

1888   Harriet composes and completes "the quilt of Adam and Eve in the Garden of Eden–afterward sold it to Mrs. Jennie Smith," according to a letter she wrote.

1890   African American lodge membership grows in Athens, Georgia as various lodges offer medical, death, and burial insurance, according to Peter Evans Schinkel's *The Negro in Athens and Clarke County, 1872–1900* master's thesis.

Many 1890 U.S. Census records are destroyed by fire.

1891   Harriet offers to sell the *Bible Quilt* to Jennie Smith, who no longer can afford the $10 selling price. Instead, Smith offers to purchase the *Bible Quilt* for $5. Powers accepts and requests to visit her quilt from time to time. Jennie Smith interviews Powers and captures the meaning of each quilt block from Powers. Smith's essay about the quilt and Powers' own words are documented on nine handwritten pages.

1893   "Work of Colored Women," a *New York Times* June 10th article reports on a needlework exhibit, including quilts by Black women, at the Chicago World's Fair.

1895   Jennie Smith exhibits the *Bible Quilt* at the Cotton States and International Exposition in Atlanta. The fair runs from September 18 to December 31. The *Bible Quilt* is displayed in the Negro Building, in an exhibit with artifacts by ex-slaves. Other quilts are included in the display. One photographer from the B.W. Kilburn Stereoview Company takes a picture of the *Bible Quilt* with a Pine Burr quilt and an appliquéd quilt of the Lord's Prayer in the background.

    Reporter Clara R. Jemison from Tuscaloosa, Alabama, another eyewitness to the *Bible Quilt*, describes the quilt on display at the Cotton States Expo for the *Chicago Daily* newspaper.

    Booker T. Washington delivers one of the Expo's opening addresses. It's easy to image Washington actually taking a moment to admire the *Bible Quilt* as he walks the aisles of the Negro Building.

    President Grover Cleveland tours the Negro Building.

    There is also a display of artwork from the Lucy Cobb Institute at the Fair. A painting of roses by Jennie Smith is included with the Cobb Institute display.

    Lorene Curtis Diver of Keokuk, Iowa attends the Expo and sees the *Bible Quilt*. She arranges for a local professional photographer to take a picture of the quilt. Diver later tries to purchase the quilt.

    In September, Jennie Smith writes a letter to Diver describing her purchase of the *Bible Quilt*.

    Harriet Powers travels to Atlanta and attends the Exposition on December 26, Negro Day. She presents "the governor of the colored department a watermelon Christmas Gift," according to a letter she wrote to Lorene Diver. The "governor" is presumably I. Garland Penn.

Dr. Charles C. Hall begins his tenure on the Board of Trustees for Atlanta University. He holds this position until his death.

1896   In January, Harriet Powers write a letter to Lorene Curtis Diver of Keokuk, Iowa providing insights into her life and experience as a quiltmaker.

1897   Tennessee Centennial Exposition opens on May 1 in Nashville. More than 1.7 million people attend the Expo, which closes on October 30. The Negro Building showcased "nearly 300 exhibits from 85 cities" (Source: Larson, page 144). Some articles have suggested one of Harriet Powers' quilts is displayed at this Expo. The author has not located any 1890s or early 1900s references to substantiate the claim that either of Harriet Powers' known quilts were displayed in Tennessee.

Charles F. McDannell, an Athens photographer, advertises his portrait studio in the local newspaper. Harriet Powers, at some point, has her picture taken at the McDannell studio.

1898   Dr. Charles Cuthbert Hall, sixth president of the Union Theological Seminary (1897–1908) and member of the Atlanta University Board of Trustees, is presented with Harriet Powers' *Pictorial Quilt* as a gift. The quilt is presumed to have been a commission by female faculty members or wives of faculty members of Atlanta University.

The Eiffel Tower opens for the International Exhibition of Paris.

1900 – 1959

1900   The U.S. Census lists Harriet Powers and her husband Armsted as the only ones at their home. The record indicates that Harriet Powers cannot read or write.

The Kodak Brownie box roll-film camera is introduced.

1904   Jennie Smith spends the summer in Paris studying art.

1908   Dr. Charles Cuthbert Hall, owner of the *Pictorial Quilt*, dies on March 25.

1909   Armsted Powers, Harriet's husband, dies on October 30.

1910   Harriet Powers dies of pneumonia on January 1 and is buried at the Gospel Pilgrim Cemetery in Athens.

Jennie Smith moves to the renovated cottage house on the grounds of the Lucy Cobb Institute.

Lucine Finch, 25, completes five years of dramatic study at the University of Chicago and appears to spend the next few years performing on the places such as New York and Massachusetts.

1912   The Colored State Fair is held in Macon, Georgia. More than 40,000 attend. Prizes for best quilts are awarded.

Lucine Finch performs and directs plays at Lake Erie College in Painesville, Ohio this year and next.

1914   "A Sermon in Patchwork" article is published in *Outlook* magazine by Lucine Finch. She describes Powers' *Bible Quilt* in the following way: "It is the reverent, worshipful embodiment of an old colored woman's soul." Later she writes: "The whole quilt is made of gay-colored calico, most beautifully quilted with the finest stitches. The border is rose colored, the spotted animals yellow and purple." It is unclear whether Finch ever met Harriet Powers in person or where she received her information and photograph of the *Bible Quilt*.

1922   Lorene Diver passes away. She is survived by her husband, James B. Diver, who passes away in 1930.

1930   Jennie Smith is honored for fifty years of service to the Lucy Cobb Institute. She is presented with a basket of flowers and gold coins worth $700.

1931   The Lucy Cobb Institute, founded in 1858, closes its doors.

Lucine Finch hosts a weekly fifteen-minute radio program "Stories of the Old South" on New York station WJZ760.

1939   Alonzo Powers, Harriet's son, is interviewed for the Folklore Project of the Federal Writers' Project, Works Progress Administration (WPA).

1946   Jennie Smith passes away on March 14 at the age of eighty-four.

Harold Milton Heckman, a forty-five-year faculty member at the University of Georgia (1921–1966) and chairman of the

University of Georgia accounting department, is named executor of Jennie Smith's estate. There is no specific instructions in Jennie's will for the *Bible Quilt*. Heckman and his wife care for the *Bible Quilt* for more than two decades.

1947   Lucine Finch passes away in Greenwich, Connecticut.

1955   Seamstress and quilter Rosa Parks refuses to give up her seat on an Alabama public bus to a white passenger. Her arrest sparks the Montgomery Bus Boycott, led by Rev. Martin Luther King, Jr. The boycott lasts 381 days, until the U.S. Supreme Court declares segregation on public buses unconstitutional.

1959   The contents of "Port Sunshine," Lorene and James Diver's home, are sold at public auction.

1960 – 1999

1960   Rev. Basil Hall personally takes the *Pictorial Quilt* to the Museum of Fine Arts, Boston and offers it for sale to the museum during a meeting with Adolph S. Cavallo, the museum's Textile Curator.

1961   Maxim Karolik purchases the *Pictorial Quilt*, though the quilt physically remains at the Museum of Fine Arts.

1963   Maxim Karolik dies on December 20.

1964   The Museum of Fine Arts, Boston accepts the bequest of Maxim Karolik of Harriet Powers' *Pictorial Quilt*.

1965   *Antiques* magazine announces the *Pictorial Quilt* acquisition.

1969   In April Harold Heckman donates the *Bible Quilt* and Jennie Smith's essay and quilt descriptions by Harriet Powers to the Smithsonian National Museum of History and Technology. According to Doris Bowman, Associate Curator at the Smithsonian Institution, "It just came in the mail and we opened it and we were just floored…It was so different from anything we had ever seen." (Source: *Atlanta Journal- Constitution*, April 4, 1999, p. M1.)

The *Bible Quilt* goes on display at the National Museum of History and Technology.

The *Washington Post* announces the display of the *Bible Quilt* at the Smithsonian. A large photo of the *Bible Quilt* is featured.

Quilter's Newsletter Magazine, one of the first professional magazines devoted to quilting, publishes its first issue.

1970 Linda Nochlin's essay "Why Have There Been No Great Women Artists" is published in *Artnews.*

1971 Adolph S. Cavallo, the former Textile Curator at the Museum of Fine Arts, Boston, is in Washington, D.C. for business. He visits the Smithsonian Museum of History and Technology and takes a moment to leisurely view the exhibits, including the famed Foucault Pendulum. A quilt near the pendulum seems familiar to him. It's the *Bible Quilt.* The place card indicates the quiltmaker's name was "Harriet," an ex-slave from Athens, GA.

Cavallo alerts Doris M. Bowman, Lace and Needlework Specialist in the Division of Textiles at the museum, that *Bible Quilt* was most likely stitched by Harriet Powers, the quilter of the *Pictorial Quilt* at the Museum of Fine Arts, Boston.

Bowman mails a photograph and description of the *Bible Quilt* to Larry Salmon, MFA Acting Curator of Textiles. Salmon provides biographical information about Powers, including her last name and birth year, and a photograph of the *Bible Quilt* to Bowman. The two known-surviving quilts by Harriet Powers are formally connected.

The groundbreaking exhibit *Abstract Design in American Quilts,* curated by Jonathan Holstein and Gail van der Hoof, opens at the Whitney Museum of American Art. This show generates unprecedented attention from the general art world for quilting. No African American-made quilts are included.

Where We At, a Black women's artists' group in New York, is founded by Kay Brown, Dindga McCannon, Faith Ringgold, and others.

1973 The Museum of Fine Arts, Boston publishes a pattern book based on the Harriet Powers quilt in its collection.

1974 *Ms.* Magazine publishes Alice Walker's essay "In Search of Our Mothers' Gardens." One passage talks about "anonymous" black women artists. She writes: "... in the Smithsonian Institution in Washington, DC, there hangs a quilt unlike any other in the world. In fanciful, inspired, and yet simple and identifiable figures, it portrays the story of the Crucifixion. It is considered rare, beyond price." Most likely, the quilt is Harriet Powers' *Bible Quilt*.

1976   Metropolitan Museum of Art displays the *Pictorial Quilt* in the exhibit *Selections of 19th Century Afro-American Art*.

Dr. Gladys-Marie Fry publishes her landmark research profiling the life of Harriet Powers in *Missing Pieces: Georgia Folk Art 1770—1976* exhibit catalog. Fry conducted the first full-scale investigation into Powers' life story.

The *Pictorial Quilt* is on display in the *Missing Pieces* exhibit. This is the first time the quilt has been available for public viewing in Georgia since the quilt was presented to Dr. Charles Cuthbert Hall in 1898.

1978   John Michael Vlach compares Harriet Powers' creative techniques to the Fon from Benin in the catalog *The Afro-American Tradition in Decorative Arts*.

Roland Freeman's quilt exhibit *Something to Keep You Warm* opens at the Old Capital Museum of Mississippi History.

1979   Cuesta Benberry creates a sampler quilt, *Afro-American Women and Quilts*, as a lecture tool to illustrate African American women's quilt history. One block represents the *Bible Quilt*.

1980   *From Fiber to Fine Arts* exhibit opens at the Museum of Fine Arts, Boston. The *Pictorial Quilt* is included.

1981   *Forever Free: Art by African American Women 1862–1980*, the largest exhibit of Black women artists, is organized by the Illinois State University. Nearly 120 works are included.

1982   Lucile DeGangi recreates the *Bible Quilt* and displays it at the West Broward Quilters Guild Show.

Ritual and Myth: A Survey of Afro-American Art opens at the Studio Museum of Harlem. The *Pictorial Quilt* is included.

"Some Do's and Don'ts for Black Women Artists" by Emma Amos is published in *Heresies, a Feminist Publication on Art and Politics*, volume 15.

1983   *Religious Folk Art in America: Reflections of Faith*, an exhibit at the American Folk Art Museum, opens. The *Pictorial Quilt* is included. A remark in the catalog suggests "another quilt similar" to Powers "has surfaced in Tennessee." No citation is included to learn more.

1987   Harold M. Heckman, the executor of Jennie Smith's estate and donor of the *Bible Quilt* to the Smithsonian, passes away.

M. Akua McDaniel publishes "Black Women: Making Quilts of Their Own" in *Art Papers* magazine, September/October.

1990   Mara R. Witzling of the University of New Hampshire compares Harriet Powers' quilt "to a work as highly positioned within the canon as Michelangelo's Sistine Chapel ceiling" during the 78th annual convention of the College Art Association in New York.

1991   The Lucy Cobb Institute in Athens is finally restored after almost seven years. It serves as the headquarters of the Carl Vinson Institute of Government.

A roundtable discussion titled "Amid the Seven Stars: A Film Project on Southern Cultural History" takes place at the University of Maryland, College Park. The film, in pre-production, is about Harriet Powers and Jennie Smith.

1992   "What Quilting Means to Black Women," a January 26th *New York Times* article by Barbara Delatiner, is published.

"Thoughts on Being a Black Quiltmaker" by Joann Thompson is published in *American Quilter*.

The Smithsonian's decision to reproduce selected nineteenth-century quilts in its collection in overseas factories sparks a national controversy. One of the quilts selected to be reproduced is Harriet Powers' 1886 *Bible Quilt*.

The *Spiegel Catalog* offers mass reproductions of the *Bible Quilt*. Prices range from $198 to $398.

The first "National Quilting Day" is celebrated on March 21.

1994   "Sweet Dreams: Bedcovers and Bed Clothes" exhibit at Museum of Fine Arts, Boston. *Pictorial Quilt* is featured.

1995   Quilt historian Cuesta Benberry is featured lecturer at the Museum of Fine Arts, Boston. Her topic is "America's Cherished Bedcovers: The Harriet Powers Bible Quilts."

Gloria Douglas, Donna Harris, and Michelle Lewis create *Storytellers in Cloth Retreats*, an annual multiple-day workshop celebrating quilting in the Black community.

1996   Joan Halimah Brooks, a descendent of Harriet Powers, produces a segment titled "A Stitch Back in Time" for the newsmagazine Real to Reel. She films several Powers family members viewing the *Pictorial Quilt* for the first time ever.

1997   Jeanne Heckman Greenleaf, Harold M. Heckman's last surviving child, passes away. She was forty-nine years old when her father donated the *Bible Quilt* to the Smithsonian. She may have been the last person alive to possibly have slept under the *Bible Quilt*.

The exhibit *Daughters of Harriet Powers* opens in St. Petersburg, Florida. Rhonda Mason is the curator.

The Seney-Stovall Chapel, built in 1882 in Athens, Georgia for the Lucy Cobb Institute, is finally restored and available for public events such as plays, weddings, and meetings.

1998   *Womenfolk*, an art exhibit at Wesleyan College in Macon, Georgia opens. Nyssa Hattaway curates this show focused on works by Georgia folk artists: Linda Anderson, Arester Earl, Yvonne Grovner, Bessie Harvey, Grace Hewell, Mattie Lou O'Kelley, Harriet Powers, Marie Rogers, Nellie Mae Rowe, Mae Tarver, Jessie Telfair, Lucinda Toomer and Lizzie Wilkerson. The show included a reproduction of the *Bible Quilt* and a photomural of the *Pictorial Quilt*.

The essay "Dispelling Myths About African-American Quilts" by Barbara E. Brown is published in the American Quilt Study Group newsletter *Blanket Statements*.

1999   *Georgia Quilts: Piecing Together History* exhibit opens at the Atlanta History Center, April 9 – June 13. The actual *Pictorial Quilt* is a featured item. This is the second time the quilt is displayed in the state of Georgia in one hundred years.

Hidden in Plain View: A Secret Story of Quilts and the Underground Railroad by Jacqueline L. Tobin and Raymond G. Dobard is published.

The Second Annual Hands and Hearts Quilt Auction, sponsored by quilters in Clark County, Washington and parts of Oregon, raises funds for a local medical team. One item auctioned is a full-size reproduction of one of Harriet Powers' Bible-themed quilts stitched by Clackamas, Oregon quilters.

2000 – 2012

2000   Jennie Smith's diary, held at the Hargrett Rare Book & Manuscript Library at the University of Georgia, is finally available to be read by the public. Harold Heckman and his wife, Claudia, donated the diary, along with other Smith papers, with the stipulation that the diary remain closed for fifty years to protect those living who may have been mentioned in the diary. The diary does not appear to mention Harriet Powers or her known quilts.

2002   The first Stitching Stars Storytelling Festival is organized by Jackie Elsner and Michael Bush of the Athens-Clarke County Library in Athens, Georgia. The festival is named after a book about Harriet Powers, *Stitching Stars* by Mary Lyons.

Mrs. Pauline Hartford gives a 1984 replica *Pictorial Quilt*, made by a group of fourteen quilters, to the Athens-Clarke County Library in March 2002 in honor of the First Annual Stitching Stars Storytelling Festival. The quilt appears to have been a fundraising prize purchased at a Friends of the University of Georgia Botanical Garden event. The quilt remains on display at the Athens-Clarke County Library.

Heart Melodies: African American Quilts Made in Georgia exhibit opens at the Spruill Gallery in Athens from January to March. The exhibit features thirty quilts including ones by Amalia Amaki, Winnie McQueen, and Phyllis Stevens. A notable quilt, Jessie Telfair's 1975 *Freedom Quilt*, is displayed. The exhibit also includes a reproduction of one of Harriet Powers' quilts, most likely the *Bible Quilt*.

2003   Grace Cavalieri's play *Quilting the Sun*, a fictional account of why Harriet Powers would sell her *Bible Quilt* to Jennie Smith, is presented at the Smithsonian Institution in Washington, D.C. Shela Xoregos directs the production.

2004   *Threads of Faith: Recent Works from the Women of Color Quilters Network*, an exhibit of fifty-three quilts opens at the

Gallery of the American Bible Society. These quilts all feature religious themes. One quilt, by Peggie Hartwell, honors Harriet Powers.

Catherine Holmes, a University of Georgia graduate student, rediscovers the graves of Harriet and Armsted Powers at the Gospel Pilgrim Cemetery in Athens, Georgia.

Karen Davis launches her blog, *Seamless Skin*, to explore creativity and quilting. This is one of the first blogs by an African American quilter; it continues today.

2005   Jennifer Gilbert, executive director of the New England Quilt Museum, lectures on "African American Quilts: From the Historical to the Innovative" at the Museum of Fine Arts, Boston. Her talk mentions Harriet Powers.

YouTube.com, a video-sharing website, is founded.

2006   The *Bible Quilt* is displayed in the exhibit "Treasures of American History" at the Smithsonian Air & Space Museum, Washington, D.C. This is the first time in thirty-seven years the *Bible Quilt* is displayed outside of the National Museum of American History. Visit YouTube.com to see the video, "Harriet Powers Bible Quilt at the Air & Space Museum in DC."

2007   *Quilting the Sun* premieres at the Centre Stage, a Greenville, SC theater. Carrie Ann Collins directs the production.

Exhibit featuring reproduction quilts by Topeka, Kansas resident Hortense Horton Beck, 87, opens at the Metropolitan Arts Council Gallery in Greenville, South Carolina. Included in the exhibit are replicas of quilts designed by Ruth Clement Bond when her husband worked for the Tennessee Valley Authority in the 1930s, *Couples* (circa 1880) by Mary Jan Batson and Mariah Chapman, *Black Family Album* (1854) by Sarah Ann Wilson, and Harriet Powers' *Pictorial Quilt*.

The essay "Black Women Have Always Quilted," by Kyra E. Hicks, is published in Elise Schebler Roberts' *The Quilt: A History and Celebration of an American Art Form.*

2008   The National Museum of American History opens in November after extensive renovations. The third floor Textile Hall is no longer in existence in the renovated museum. The *Bible Quilt* remains in the museum's Textile Collection storage room.

Harriet Powers' headstone at the Gospel Pilgrim Cemetery in Athens, Georgia is found damaged.

Laurel Thatcher Ulrich of Harvard University lectures on "A Quilt Unlike Any Other: Rediscovering the Work of Harriet Powers" at the University of Mississippi as part of Women's History Month celebrations.

2009   A copy of a letter from Harriet Powers, in Lorene Curtis Diver's handwriting, is rediscovered in the Lee County Historical Society files in Keokuk, Iowa. Harriet Powers' words change many of our perceptions of this nineteenth-century quilter. There is also a copy of a letter from Jennie Smith, also in Diver's handwriting, in the files.

Harriet Powers is one of three women inducted into the Georgia Women of Achievement Hall of Fame at its 18th annual ceremony at Wesleyan College in Macon.

William "Bill" Gilcher lectures on Harriet Powers and the *Bible Quilt* at St. Andrew's Episcopal Church in College Park, Maryland. Gilcher is a long-time Powers researcher.

Tommy30507, a Georgia artist, shares how Harriet Powers inspired his paintings via a YouTube.com video titled "Suns and Suns and Suns."

Synton House, where the *Pictorial Quilt* once hung, opens again in Westport Point, Massachusetts for summer renters.

The Athens (GA) Historical Society celebrates its 50th anniversary.

2010   The *Pictorial Quilt* is anticipated to be on exhibit for the first time in nearly nine years when the Museum of Fine Arts, Boston opens its new American Wing.

2012   This is the 185th anniversary of Harriet Powers' birth.

Further Areas for Explorations

Isn't it amazing how much Harriet Powers' quilts continue to fascinate us more than one hundred years after she finished stitching them? There are, however, a few areas I feel are still ripe for exploration, celebration and research.

1. **HARRIET POWERS' TWO KNOWN QUILTS TOUR THE UNITED STATES TOGETHER FOR THE FIRST TIME.** I've seen the *Bible Quilt* on display at the Smithsonian at least a dozen times over as many years. In 2006, I even had the pleasure of seeing the quilt in storage—being close enough to touch the same fibers Harriet Powers touched. In May 2008, I had the honor of seeing the *Pictorial Quilt* up-close at the Museum of Fine Arts in Boston. To the best of my research, these quilts have not been on display in the same exhibit—ever. As a quilter, it's a moving moment to be in the presence of Harriet Powers' work. How awesome it would be to visit a museum to see both quilts on display in the same room!

2. **DEFINITIVE BIOGRAPHY OF HARRIET POWERS IS PUBLISHED.** We need a fresh look at Harriet Powers' life story through the lens of her nineteenth-century African American community and social history in Athens, Georgia. What was Black life like in Athens during this time? Who were her neighbors? What churches, besides Mt. Zion Baptist Church, did she and her family attend? Was she or her husband a member of a local Athens lodge? Was it unusual that Mrs. Powers owned land? Did many other Black women in Athens also own land? What are the details of the Athens Colored Fairs? Is there other evidence Harriet Powers exhibited her quilts at one of the annual Fairs? Did any of Powers daughters, granddaughters or great-grand daughters quilt?

3. **FIND HARRIET POWERS' *LORD'S SUPPER QUILT*.** In Powers' 1896 letter to Lorene Curtis Diver, she mentioned that sometime after 1882 she "composed a quilt of the Lord's Supper from the New Testament. 2 thousand and 5 hundred diamonds." This is not the *Bible Quilt*, which she refers to as the "Adam and Eve in the Garden of Eden" quilt. Nor is it the *Pictorial Quilt,* which does not include imagery of

the Lord's Supper. Two of Powers' quilts have independently survived more than 100 years. Is it possible her *Lord's Supper Quilt* has also survived and is in a private or public collection today? Are there any clues as to what Harriet Powers meant by "2 thousand and 5 hundred diamonds?" Did she sew the three layers of the *Lord's Supper Quilt* with a diamond pattern? Are the diamonds a unit of measurement? Can we determine what happened to the *Lord's Supper Quilt*?

4. **UNCOVER MORE FIRST-PERSON ACCOUNTS FROM THOSE WHO TOUCHED THE *BIBLE QUILT* OR THE *PICTORIAL QUILT*.** I screamed and cried when my eyes fell upon the copy of the letter written by Harriet Powers to Lorene Diver in 1896. Until February 2009, no one interested in quilt history even knew the copy of the Harriet Powers or Jennie Smith letters existed. The copy of the Powers letter and her photograph taken at the McDannell studio have patiently waited in a file for more than three decades to be rediscovered. What other letters or diary entries still patiently await to be found? Did Mrs. Jeanie Hall write in a journal about her husband receiving the *Pictorial Quilt* in 1898? Did Rev. Basil Hall write about selling it in his diary? Are there any other surviving papers of Maxim Karolik with notes about the quilt? Are there any additional papers about the *Bible Quilt* from Harold Heckman or Anne Brumby?

Thirty-thousand people attended Negro Day, December 26, 1895, at the Cotton States and International Exposition in Atlanta, including Harriet Powers. Did reporters from the nation's Black newspapers, such as the *Washington Bee,* the Indianapolis *Freeman*, the St. Paul *Broad Ax* or the AME *Review*, file a story about the day, or about their impressions of the needlearts on display? Several Black colleges exhibited at the Exposition. Are there college records or student newspaper articles about the needleart displays? Did prominent African Americans in attendance possibly write about meeting Harriet Powers in letters or diaries that may have survived?

Finally, perhaps a film crew will record the oral histories from museum curators who have cared for both Powers quilts these last four decades. For example, Doris Bowman at the Smithsonian opened the box that contained the *Bible Quilt* when it arrived at that museum. Adolph Cavallo, former Textile Curator at the Museum of Fine Arts,

Boston, accepted the *Pictorial Quilt* from Rev. Basil Hall. What a unique perspective they will have!

5. **DETERMINE WHETHER LORENE CURTIS DIVER COMMISSIONED A QUILT FROM HARRIET POWERS.** Did correspondence between Lorene Diver and Harriet Powers stop after only one letter? Did Mrs. Diver commission a quilt from Mrs. Powers? We know the terms of James Diver's will prohibited the sale of Port Sunshine, the home he shared with his wife, Lorene, or its contents. An auction of the home's items did eventually take place on September 19, 1959, nearly thirty years after Mr. Diver passed away. Are there any records about the inventory or buyers from the auction? Did the local newspaper or the estate's Trustee record the event or its outcome? We know an eleven-year-old girl purchased a sewing machine for a quarter at the auction. Is there anyone today in or from Keokuk, Iowa who remembers the auction? Were there any quilts, possibly an appliquéd story quilt by Harriet Powers, sold that day?

Did Raymond Garrison (1890–1980), the local Keokuk historian who had the copy of the Harriet Powers letter, have any additional notes about Mrs. Diver or Mrs. Powers? Are there any written or oral histories about the Divers' trip to the 1895 Exposition in Atlanta or the encounter with Harriet Powers' *Bible Quilt* known to members of the Diver or Curtis extended families today?

6. **HOST SYMPOSIUM ON HARRIET POWERS AND HER QUILTS IN 2012.** Let's take time to celebrate the 185th anniversary of her birth by coming together in discussion of her life and her artwork.

7. **PUBLISH PATTERN BOOK FOR BOTH KNOWN POWERS QUILTS.**

8. **U.S. POSTAL SERVICE ISSUES A HARRIET POWERS COMMEMORATIVE STAMP.** For the 185th anniversary of her birth in 2012, could there be a postage stamp? One can petition the U.S. Postal Service to issue a Harriet Powers Commemorative stamp by writing to: The Citizens Stamp Advisory Committee, c/o Stamp Development, U.S. Postal Service, 1735 North Lynn St., Suite 5013, Arlington, VA 22209.

9. **HARRIET POWERS' FINAL RESTING PLACE IS PRESERVED.** Today, the exact location of Harriet Powers' headstone at the Gospel Pilgrim Cemetery in Athens, Georgia is not published for fear of vandals disturbing the fragile headstone. In late 2008, Harriet Powers' headstone was found damaged. It is hoped the location of Powers and her husband's final resting place will be fully restored.

10. **COMPREHENSIVE REVIEW OF THE SMITHSONIAN QUILT CONTROVERSY.** Licensing of well-known artwork is common today. When the *Bible Quilt* design was licensed to create affordable quilts for the public in 1991—92, there was an uproar among thousands of quilters. More than fifteen years have passed, enough time for reflective contemplation of the controversy. Here are the questions I'd like to have insight into:
   - What are the feelings today of Smithsonian officials, American Pacific management, and quilters involved in the controversy?
   - How many quilt designs were finally made by American Pacific Enterprises, which had the right to reproduce twelve Smithsonian historical quilts?
   - Each Smithsonian quilt came with a registration card. How many quilts were finally registered? What benefits, if any, were provided to those who registered their quilts?
   - What is the secondary market value for the reproduced quilts?
   - What happened to the American Quilt Defense Fund? Is it still active today?
   - Are there papers, letters, petition copies, or newspaper or magazine articles from the controversy saved in any library repository? If so, where?
   - When pillows featuring blocks of the *Pictorial Quilt* were produced in 2001 by the Museum of Fine Arts, Boston, was there a similar outcry from some quilters? Why? Why not?
   - What were the lasting effects, if any, of the controversy at the Smithsonian and for other major quilt collections nationally?

11. **EXHIBIT HARRIET POWERS'** *PICTORIAL QUILT* **IN THE CONTEXT OF THE KAROLIK COLLECTIONS.** The M. and M. Karolik Collections are among the most renowned in U.S. museum and art worlds. How fantastic it would be to see the *Pictorial Quilt* displayed with other

iconic pieces in the Karolik Collections or exhibited with all other objects with African American imagery in the Karolik Collections.

12. **WHO DONATED LORENE DIVER'S 1895-96 "SERMON IN PATCHWORK" PHOTOGRAPH TO THE SMITHSONIAN INSTITUTION?** The existence of Lorene Diver's *Bible Quilt* photograph at the National Museum of American History led to the eventual discovery of the copy of the letter by accomplished woman Harriet Powers. As of May 2009, the Smithsonian Institution has not been able to locate the physical document(s) confirming who donated the photograph. Oral history suggests that an institution in Alabama, the state where Lucine Finch grew up, gave the photograph to the museum since the Smithsonian owned the *Bible Quilt*. I believe this documentation may yield as yet undiscovered insights into the larger Powers story:

- Are there other Lorene Diver photographs from 1895-96? What would they show? Who would they show?
- Is there a tangible connection between the "Sermon in Patchwork" photograph, Lorene Diver and Lucine Finch?
- How did an institution in Alabama get a photograph owned by a woman in Keokuk, Iowa?
- What connection, if any, did the well-traveled Lorene Diver have with Alabama?
- Are there other people, as yet unknown, who may hold additional keys to information about Harriet Powers and her quilts?

Oh! There is always one last thread to pull, one more lead to follow! I hope the information in this book will help a curious quilt detective, local historian, a librarian, a family genealogist, an ambitious undergrad or grad student, or maybe even you locate new leads and evidence about Harriet Powers' life and her quilts.

What an adventure that will be!

Mrs. Harriet Powers, pencil drawing, 2008
By Zoe Madison Waller
Age 13

This drawing is reprinted with the artist's, and her mother's, permission.

About the Author

Kyra E. Hicks is a quilter. Her quilts have appeared in more than forty exhibits in the United States and abroad. She loves historical, investigative research and rediscovering the lives of quilters past. She is the author of *Black Threads: An African American Quilting Sourcebook* (2003) and the children's book *Martha Ann's Quilt for Queen Victoria* (2007). She co-authored *Liberia: A Visit Through Books* (2008) with Izetta Roberts Cooper. Kyra hosts a blog on African American quilting news- www.BlackThreads.blogspot.com.

Kyra holds an MBA from the University of Michigan, a diploma from the London School of Economics and Political Science, and a BBA from Howard University. She currently works for Marriott International and lives in Arlington, Virginia, where she tends her colorful, fragrant rose garden.

Author's Note

I hope you enjoyed this book! Do feel free to drop me a note or let me know if you'd like to be on my mailing list when my next book is published. I'll give you a hint – it's also on African American quilting!

Kyra E. Hicks
3037 S. Buchanan Street
Arlington, VA 22206-1512

More Books by Kyra E. Hicks

Black Threads: An African American Quilting Sourcebook
ISBN: 0-7864-1374-3

Black Threads is a comprehensive guide to African American quilt history and contemporary practices. It offers over 1,700 bibliographic references from books, articles, exhibit catalogs, and more. Also included are quilt industry estimates, a listing of African American-made quilts in 100 museums, survey results of African American quilter fabric purchasing and quiltmaking practices, and an extensive timeline covering 200 years of African American quilt history.

More Books by Kyra E. Hicks

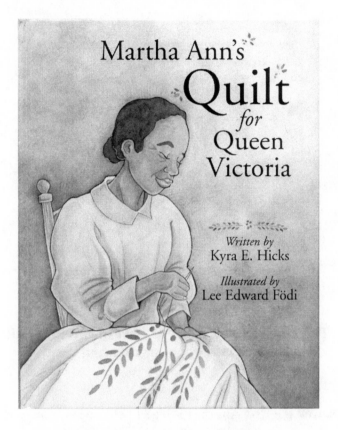

Martha Ann's Quilt for Queen Victoria
ISBN: 1-933285-59-1

Martha Ann is twelve years old when Papa finally purchases her freedom from slavery and moves the family from Tennessee to Liberia. On Market Days, Martha Ann watches the British navy patrolling the Liberian coast to stop slave catchers from kidnapping family and neighbors and forcing them back into slavery.

Martha Ann decides to thank Queen Victoria in person for sending the navy. But first, she has to save money for the 3,500 mile voyage, find a suitable gift for the queen, and withstand the ridicule of those who learn of her impossible dream to meet the Queen of England. A true story!

49¢ Short eEssay by Kyra E. Hicks

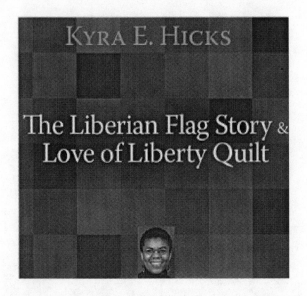

The Liberian Flag Story & Love of Liberty Quilt
Available exclusively on Amazon.com – only 49¢

Who sewed the first American flag? I bet you said Betsy Ross.

Who sewed the first Liberian flag? In 1847, seven Black American women, who emigrated from the United States to Liberia, met at the home of Susannah Waring Lewis to sew. Their project, this time, was not a quilt. Instead, they had the honor of stitching their new nation's first national flag.

Read more about Susannah Waring Lewis, Sarah Draper, Mrs. Mary L. Hunter, Mrs. Rachel Johnson, Mrs. Matilda Newport., Mrs. J. B. Russwurm, and Collinette Teage Ellis. The flag design these nineteenth century friends stitched in 1847 is the same flag design under which Ellen Johnson Sirleaf, the first woman President of Liberia, took the oath of office under in 2006.

A bonus *Love of Liberty Quilt* pattern is included.

LaVergne, TN USA
26 December 2010

210038LV00016B/156/P